TITLE PAGE

Text Copyright © 2007 by OutstandingeBooks, Inc.

Illustrations Copyright © 2007 by OutstandingeBooks, Inc.

Kirsner, Craig

The Art Of Telling Great Jokes & Being Funny ☺

by Craig Kirsner

ISBN # 978-0-6151-4503-7

Cover design by Carla Cid De Diego

First Printing April 2007

Manufactured in the United States of America

Copyright information next page

COPYRIGHT PAGE

DISCLAIMER

This eBook contains politically incorrect and adult jokes and graphic material that might be considered offensive by some.

By reading this eBook, you certify that you are over the age of 18 (eighteen) and are not offended by adult humor.

If you are under age 18 then please do not read the content of this eBook.

All of the jokes inside this eBook were either sent to me or found on numerous sites on the Internet. I believe they are all public domain jokes, however, if any of these jokes are copyrighted please contact me and I will remove it or give proper credit.

10% of all net profits are donated to <u>Miami's Community Partnership for Homeless</u> to feed the homeless.

Thank you for your purchase.

ACKNOWLEDGEMENT:

I want to acknowledge my family for their ongoing support as well as my good friends. I especially want to thank Rene for getting me started down this path and Maria for supporting me along the way.

I want to share a few jokes that my little brother Geoffrey told me, as he is only 13:

What do you call a female tortoise?
A clitortoise! ☺

What do you call a lesbian dinosaur?
A Lickolotopus! ☺

Thanks Geoff! I love you!

FREE BONUS FOR READERS OF THIS EBOOK!!

Each week I send the best 2 – 3 jokes I receive during the week, and you can get them too for free.
Sign up by going here (your email address will be kept safe):
https://app.quicksizzle.com/survey.aspx?sfid=18767

TABLE OF CONTENTS

INTRODUCTION – Page 6

- Friday Funnies! - How I got into joke telling
- George Castanza needed me!
- Breakthrough Memory Technique to remember the jokes
- An example of a picture reminding you of a joke
- What kind of joke teller are you?

PART 1: TECHNIQUES TO TELL A GREAT JOKE – 11

- The secret to humor – the setup of the joke
- The punchline of a joke
- Punchline examples
- Know your audience
- Be relaxed and confident
- Timing
- Keep the opposite sex laughing
- "Hey Now" – funny phrases to use
- Warning – Never oversell a joke
- Practice

PART 2: THE BEST JOKES I HAVE EVER HEARD – 20

PART 3: GREAT CLEAN JOKES – 27

PART 4: GREAT POLITICALLY INCORRECT JOKES–79

PART 5: BLOND JOKES – 120

PART 6: SNAPS! – 133

PART 7: ETC. (MORE FUNNY THINGS) – 138

PART 8: THE FUNNIEST SITES ON THE NET – 145

INTRODUCTION

JOKES!!!

Jokes are great icebreakers, confidence builders and a recipe for a good time!

But many people usually can't remember their favorite jokes and others don't feel like they can successfully tell jokes. I am here to tell you that this eBook finally solves both of those issues.

The first part of this eBook discusses how to tell jokes successfully. The second part of this eBook gives you great jokes and most importantly an easy way to remember these jokes. And not only are they the greatest jokes out there, but there are jokes for every occasion!

Who am I to tell you these jokes? I am no stand up comedian, but I am known amongst my friends as the man with the jokes, the guy that can make anyone laugh! (and also as the man with the dirty jokes – don't worry, I will give you plenty of both kinds!)

FRIDAY FUNNIES! – HOW I GOT INTO JOKES

Where do I get my jokes? Each week I get about 10 – 50 jokes sent to me via email or text message from friends, as most people do, and the majority of these jokes are cute but are not very funny. The few jokes that are really funny I keep and send to my friends via email every Friday. I call this email "Friday Funnies" and they contain the best 2 – 3 jokes I receive all week. I have become well known for my "Friday Funnies" email.

I have been sending out the "Friday Funnies" email just about every Friday for numerous years. I find when I don't send out my Friday Funnies some people actually complain! One of my best friends Rene told me a couple of years ago that he was sitting at his office on a Friday afternoon with some co-workers and they wanted to hear a joke. He told his colleagues that his friend Craig sends out great jokes by email every Friday so he went to his email and found– NO JOKES! I guess I was too busy that day and he was a bit pissed off! So I make it a point to send them every week now. People rely on me for good laughs and I don't disappoint them.

The Friday Funnies email showed me that people really need a constant supply of good jokes. Everyone wants to laugh and more importantly people enjoy making others laugh.

Jokes are a way to relieve stress, break ice, and even build bonds. However, I also came to realize that sometimes a steady supply of jokes doesn't guarantee that someone will be able to tell a joke well.

"GEORGE COSTANZA" NEEDED ME!

While most of us love to hear a good joke, not all of us can deliver jokes well. I'm sure you, like me, sat around at some point trying to remember a great joke or worse told a joke only to hear nothing but crickets.

I also thought of somebody like 'George Costanza' from Seinfeld and thought that he could really have used someone as a 'joke coach' to help him 'make friends' and be more personable

.

Then I realized there are many people who could use this kind of advice.
Perhaps they are shy, had told a bad joke in the past or simply can't remember a good joke.

Well, I want to help those people out!

BREAKTHROUGH MEMORY TECHNIQUE TO REMEMBER THE JOKES

Years ago I learned a memory technique to remember anything easily. When you want to remember something what you need to do is:

- Create a picture in your mind. This picture should remind you of the joke or thing that you are trying to remember.
- The last part of the memory trick is that the picture should have action involved for maximum memory retention.

Let me give you some examples of how this works in real life:

If you want to learn a foreign language, for example, Spanish, and you want to remember that the Spanish word for cow is "vaca", you imagine a cow standing up, vacuuming the pasture. Vacuum will remind you of "vaca". This language memory trick comes in handy when living in Miami, Florida, as I do!

Also, if you need to make a left at the street with an Exon gas station on it, you picture the Exon gas station with leaves blowing through it (leaves = left), perhaps the leaves are on fire, and the Exon gas station is about to BLOW UP!

These memory secrets will help you remember the jokes, because each joke has a picture next to it that will 'jog' your memory when you need to remember the joke.

Then you will find yourself in a conversation and something will come up (I.E. a bunny rabbit) and you will start to picture the bunny joke pictures in your imagination and you will have a number of jokes at your fingertips that will keep them laughing!

AN EXAMPLE OF A PICTURE REMINDING YOU OF THE JOKE:

Why won't a blond girl
make a good cattle herder?

*Because she can't even
keep her two calves together!* ☺

Get it? Two calves? LOL So that's an example of a picture reminding you of a joke. I bet you will NEVER forget that one! Every time I think of that joke I smile ☺

WHAT TYPE OF JOKE TELLER ARE YOU?

You must know your funny strengths. Please find below a list of potential types of comics you could be:

- Street Comic – you can point out the humor in life and other people
- Living Room Comic – you are funny in the living room only
- Regurgitating Comic – you can repeat a joke really well
- Too Late Comic – you think of funny things later
- 9 Times Out Of 10 Comic – you say funny things, but it's that last one that kills you
- Copy Cat Comic – you copy great comedians, like Jerry Seinfeld

The point is to figure out what type of comic you are, and work with your strengths. In the next section you will find what makes a joke funny and actually what humor is. This will make you a better street comic. Then you will get the jokes to become a better regurgitating comic. You can combine all of the different techniques to make yourself a funnier person overall.

So let's get started with how to tell the jokes, and then afterwards you will get the great jokes and the pictures that will help you remember the jokes.

I hope you enjoy this eBook, that it makes you laugh, and most importantly it helps you become a great joke teller and makes your friends, family and co-workers laugh!

PART 1 –
TECHNIQUES TO TELL A GREAT JOKE!

How to tell a joke – Everything you need to know except the jokes! (The jokes are in Part II through Part V, along with an easy way to remember the jokes, but no peeking!)

The intention of this section is to make you a great joke teller through learning the secrets of humor and practicing telling jokes on a regular basis.

Being a great joke teller is all about timing and confidence. The good part of this is that the more you tell jokes, the better your timing will become, and the better your timing gets, the more confidence you will have! It is a circle that works in a nice, positive way.

The other important aspect of great joke telling is that you have to be relaxed at all times. By telling jokes, you are simply adding some fun to life and your conversations – don't put too much pressure on yourself. Keep it light and easy, not too serious.

THE SECRET TO HUMOR - THE SETUP OF A JOKE

What makes a good joke? The most important part of a joke is the setup of the joke. The setup is the introductory story you tell, before telling the punchline. The setup should lead you

in one direction to expect something, and then the punchline of a joke should surprise you with something completely different.

THE PUNCHLINE OF A JOKE

When you tell the punchline of a joke, it should be short and filled with an unexpected action. That is the essence of humor, having the punchline be the opposite of what you expect to hear. In this book, all of the punchlines are *in italics*, with a smiley face ☺ after the punchline (to remind you to smile!).

PUNCHLINE EXAMPLES

Here is an example of a setup in life that leads to a funny point. Recently, I was at a famous hotel on Collins Avenue in Miami Beach when I saw this really cool desk for the valet that was made out of a plane engine:

So I said to the girl I was with, that's a great table, but *don't push that button or this guy will fly away!* ☺

This is an example of making a joke out of an every day object. You can do this with anything, or anyone. Often, humor is simply realizing what people assume about something (the setup), and saying the opposite (the punchline).

Another time I was speaking with a friend of mine and she said that she was going to a city in Florida named Davie for a kickboxing practice event. Now, Davie is a rural town with a lot of horses. So I said, "You're going to beat up a horse?" to which she started laughing out loud. Then I followed with "Stop the insanity" and kept her laughing. We proceeded to joke about other barnyard animals being beaten up and had a good time.

Or one time I was on line at the entrance to a networking event and it was taking quite a long time. When it was my turn to check in and get my parking ticket validated my ticket was stamped with a "6" three times. So I said *what do I have to pay $18?* ☺ Everyone laughed and it lightened the mood. The ticket stamper and I became good friends too after that little icebreaker as well.

Another time I was with some friends and they were talking about an island that had monkeys living on it that were raised by the government for experiments. It turns out that they had to kill many of the monkeys because they were breeding too quickly. My friend said "that was a waste of money". I replied *"that was a waste of monkey!"* ☺ The point is that the punchline leads you to a place that you were not expecting. So start looking at what's around you and you will find the humor.

KNOW YOUR AUDIENCE

Another important aspect of joke telling is to feel out the crowd and get an idea of what they would like. Some people think that it's okay to say what's on their mind, but there is a difference between funny and obnoxious. It is vital to know your crowd and know that line to not cross (but put a toe or two over it!).

Clearly a bunch of drunk people at a bar are an easier audience then those at a church convention or meeting (many of these jokes are not really appropriate for the latter!)

So feel 'em out, and see what they want. I have divided the jokes into four sections:

1. The Best Jokes I have ever heard
2. Clean Jokes
3. Politically Incorrect Jokes
4. Blonde Jokes

The very first section is a chapter with the best jokes that I have ever heard.

The second section, "Clean Jokes", contains jokes that you could tell at a church meeting and the "Politically Incorrect Jokes" contains jokes you could tell at a bar, and never the two shall meet! Just kidding, they could meet; it really depends on the crowd.

The advantage that you have over a professional comedian is that you know your audience. You know if they will get a joke or not, if they will like a joke or not, and if the joke is so offensive that it might piss them off. You will know what is appropriate; just go with your gut!

Don't worry; there are more politically incorrect jokes than clean ones, as this seems to be what gets me the greatest laughs! ;-)

Some people like to come up with their own

jokes, and if you do then it is really important that you keep it short and finish right on the punchline. Be sure and write the joke so that when you are finished with the punchline of the joke you stop talking. Let the people laugh, without continuing to tell the joke. Keep practicing at this, the more you do it the better you will get. And please send these jokes to me at craig@outstandingebooks.com

BE RELAXED AND CONFIDENT

After you have picked some great jokes and memorized them, practice them in a mirror. Think James Dean cool, confident, not caring what the outcome is, and you will have the best response. When telling a joke don't worry about a thing, stay relaxed and give it everything you've got.

Keep practicing, perhaps even in front of a video camera, so that you can watch your mannerisms and body language.

When you are telling a joke or a story you should always look happy, because if you don't look happy people will not want to hear it. Also, be animated and energetic as it will make your stories more interesting and people will focus and listen carefully to what you are saying. Finally, always be aware of your timing…

TIMING

Being relaxed is the primary most important part of joke telling, and the second most important part is timing. It is really important to get the timing of the joke down. Often, after I tell the body of a joke, and am about to tell the punchline, I pause for a brief second and look around at the audience.

I pick someone who looks like they are really listening and enjoying the joke thus far and I tell them the punchline with emphasis and then look around at the other people. In this eBook I have italicized every punch line so you can be sure to know what you need to emphasize.

I often laugh at my own jokes along with the crowd – some people say not to but I say screw 'em! I laugh as much as others and it makes me happy to do so. Just be sure and wait until after telling the punchline to start laughing.

KEEP THE OPPOSITE SEX LAUGHING

I will even use jokes when I meet a woman. Women love to feel an emotional connection and making them laugh is one great way to do that. Just keep the jokes clean in the beginning until you feel out the kind of girl you are talking to. If she likes the Politically Incorrect Jokes, she is my kind of girl! Haha

And women, let me tell you that guys like a woman who keeps us laughing and having fun. Life is too short to be with someone that is too serious all the time. Use jokes to keep things light and cheery… you will be surprised at the results!

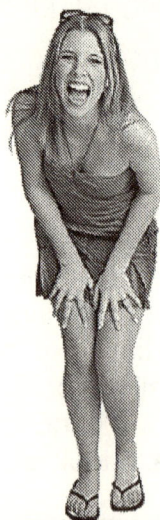

"HEY NOW!" - FUNNY PHRASES TO USE

Another way to be humorous is having a supply of funny sayings that you use in conversation to keep things light. These sayings can come from movies, TV, or famous radio personalities.

Some of my favorites include:

- "Hey Now" said with emphasis on the "now".
- "How U Doin?", with the response of "I'm Doin Baby, I'm Doin".
- Fugettaboutit.
- Great Success! (using a foreign accent)

The point is that funny phrases like these lighten up the situation, and that is really what you are going for.

In Miami, I have some funny words in multiple languages to keep my Latin friends laughing. Some Spanish words include:

- Ay Dios Mios (don't pronounce the "s"): Oh my G-d
- Cerveza: Beer
- Conjo (jo sounds like yo): it is used like the word F-ck in English.

I also know some Portuguese words for the many Brazilians I come across. Some Portuguese words that make Brazilians smile include:

- Tudo Bem, Tudo Bom, Tudo Joya (tudo sounds like tutu, Bem = baym): 3 cute ways to ask how are you, especially when said in together in a row
- Gostoza (goshtoza): a beautiful woman
- Bom Pracalio: when something is good as f-ck!
- Bom Gia (geea): Good morning
- Bom Nuiti (neweechee): Good night

Again the main point is to keep 'em smiling by keeping them off guard with a punchline that they are not expecting.

WARNING: NEVER OVERSELL A JOKE

One last thing, never oversell a joke – IE don't say "this is the funniest joke" because the expectation will be too high. Just be confident it is a funny joke as it must be if you heard it and want to repeat it!

Also, anytime someone builds up a joke like 'this is the greatest joke ever', don't bother telling it because you set yourself up for failure – the expectations are too high in that situation as well.

For example, I was on a camping trip recently and my friend Risa asks me in front of a group of 20 people to tell the great joke about Snoop Dogg.

So I say "Why does Snoop Dogg always carry an umbrella? Wait for the punchline a few seconds….
"Fo Drizzle" ☺

Not many people laughed and then she says "No, that's not the way to say it right".

The point is that the buildup was too great for the joke. I should have said something like "that is too much buildup for the joke, you tell it" or I could have told the joke later when people weren't expecting it.

By the way, the picture to remember that joke is:

PRACTICE

Last but certainly not least, if you ever want to do something new in your life, studies have shown that if you do it every day for 21 days it will be ingrained in you after that much practice.

So here is your assignment. For the next 21 days, tell at least one joke a day, ideally to 10 different people, and also pick two or three of your favorite jokes, don't tell the exact same one over and over again.

Practice makes perfect. Remember, as long as you are confident, even if you don't get the joke exactly right it will come across well!

Read through the next section, circle some jokes you really like and memorize them and most importantly their picture. You will do great!

PART 2:
THE BEST JOKES I HAVE EVER HEARD!

The next part of telling a great joke is having a variety of great jokes! This is the area where we see this all come to life! These are the best jokes I have ever heard! Enjoy!

What do you say to a woman with no arms and no legs?

Nice tits! ☺

What's the best form of birth control after 50?

Nudity ☺

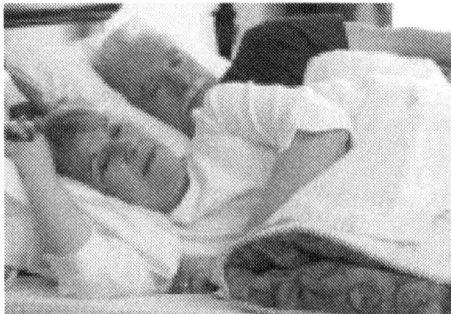

What's the difference between a girlfriend and a wife?

45 pounds ☺

What's the difference between a boyfriend and a husband?

45 minutes ☺

Why does the bride always wear white?

Because it's good for the dishwasher to match the stove and refrigerator ☺

Which sexual position produces the ugliest children?

Ask your Mom ☺

Why does Mike Tyson cry during sex?

Mace will do that to you ☺

Why did OJ Simpson want to move to West Virginia?

Everyone has the same DNA ☺

What would you call it when an Italian has one arm shorter than the other?

A speech impediment ☺

Why do men find it difficult to make eye contact?

Breasts don't have eyes ☺

What's the difference between a Southern zoo, and a Northern zoo?

A Southern zoo has a description of the animal on the front of the cage, along with the recipe ☺

What's the Cuban National Anthem?

Row, row, row, your boat ☺

An 80-year-old woman was arrested for shoplifting.
When she went before the judge he asked her, "What did you steal?" She replied: a can of peaches.
 The judge asked her why she had stolen them and she replied that she was hungry.

 The judge then asked her how many peaches were in the can. She replied 6.

The judge then said, "I will give you 6 days in jail."

 Before the judge could actually pronounce the punishment the woman's husband spoke up and asked the judge if he could say something.

 He said," What is it? "

The husband said, "She also stole a can of peas." ☺

A white woman was having a baby at the hospital and the baby's head comes out, and the head is black.

The doctor pops his head up and says "Have you ever slept with a black man?"

The woman thinks for a second and then says "Yes, once."

The doctor puts his head down, and continues. The body of the baby comes out, and it is red.

The doctor pops his head up again and says "Have you ever slept with an American Indian man?"

The woman thinks for a second and then says "Yes, once."

The doctor puts his head down again and the legs of the baby come out and they are yellow.

The doctor pops his head up again and says "Have you ever slept with an Asian man?"

The woman thinks for a second and then says "Yes, once."

The doctor picks the baby up, slaps the baby on the ass and it starts to cry.

The woman wipes her forehead and says

"Whew, I am glad he didn't bark!"☺

On their wedding night, the young bride approached her new husband and asked for $20.00 for their first lovemaking encounter. In his highly aroused state, her husband readily agreed.

This scenario was repeated each time they made love, for more than 30 years, with him thinking that it was a cute way for her to afford new clothes and other incidentals that she needed.

Arriving home around noon one day, she was surprised to find her husband in a very drunken state. During the next few minutes, he explained that his employer was going through a process of corporate downsizing, and he had been let go. It was unlikely that, at the age of 59, he'd be able to find another position that paid anywhere near what he'd been earning, and therefore, they were financially ruined.

Calmly, his wife handed him a bank book which showed more than thirty years of steady deposits and interest totaling nearly $1 million. Then she showed him certificates of deposits issued by the bank which were worth over $2 million, and informed him that they were one of the largest depositors in the bank.

She explained that for the more than three decades she had "charged" him for sex, these holdings had multiplied and these were the results of her savings and investments.

Faced with evidence of cash and investments worth over $3 million, her husband was so astounded he could barely speak, but finally he found his voice and blurted out, "If I'd had any idea what you were doing, I would have given you all my business!"

That's when she shot him. ☺

You know, sometimes, men just don't know when to keep their mouths shut.

Please email your favorite jokes to craig@outstandingebooks.com for the next edition of the Joke eBook!

PART 3:
<u>GREAT CLEAN JOKES!</u>

Don't forget to sign up for the Friday Funnies email so that every Friday you get new jokes to add to your repertoire. Go to the free signup at https://app.quicksizzle.com/survey.aspx?sfid=18767 or at www.outstandingebooks.com. Remember, we will never sell or give out your email to others.

What is do a Texas Divorce and a Texas twister have in common?

Either way, someone is losing a mobile home! ☺

What is the difference between a man and a piece of cheese?

Cheese matures with age ☺

A three-year old boy was examining his testicles while taking a bath.

"Mom", he asked, "are these my brains?"

"Not yet," She replied ☺

G-d says to Adam, "I have some good news and some bad news. What do you want to hear first?"

Adam says, "Tell me the good news first."
G-d says, "I'm going to give you a penis and a brain. You'll derive from these great pleasure and great intellect."

Adam replies, "Wonderful! But what's the bad news?"

G-d says, "I'm only going to give you enough blood supply to work one at a time." ☺

A young boy, about eight years old, was at the store picking up a large box of laundry detergent. The grocer walked over and asked the boy if he had a lot of laundry to do.

"Oh, no laundry" the boy said "I'm going to wash my dog."

"But you shouldn't use this to wash your dog. It's very powerful and it might make your dog sick or even kill him."

But the boy was not stopped by this and paid for the detergent even as the grocer continued to talk him out of it.

About a week later the boy was back in the store and the grocer asked about the dog. "Oh, he died," the boy said.

The grocer said, "I tried to tell you not to use that detergent on your dog."

"Well," the boy replied, "I don't think it was the detergent that killed him."

"Oh I'm sorry. How did he die?"

"I think it was the spin cycle" ☺

A man goes to a pastor and offers to repaint the church for $500. The pastor agrees.

The man then takes one gallon of paint, and uses thinner to make 5 gallons of paint and paints the church.

The pastor is about to pay the $500 when all of a sudden a black cloud forms over the church. It rains so hard that the paint comes off.

Then a voice comes out from the sky and says to the painter:

Repaint and thin no more! ☺

An exasperated mother, whose son was always getting into mischief, finally asked him, "How do you expect to get into Heaven?" The boy thought it over and said,

"Well, I'll run in and out and in and out and keep slamming the door until St. Peter says,
'For Heaven's sake, Dylan, come in or stay out!'" ☺

One night, as a couple lays down for bed, the husband gently taps his wife on the shoulder and starts rubbing her arm.

The wife turns over and says "I'm sorry honey, I've got a gynecologist appointment tomorrow and I want to stay fresh." The husband, rejected, turns over and tries to sleep.

A few minutes later, he rolls back over and taps his wife again. This time he whispers in her ear,

"Do you have a dentist appointment tomorrow too?" ☺

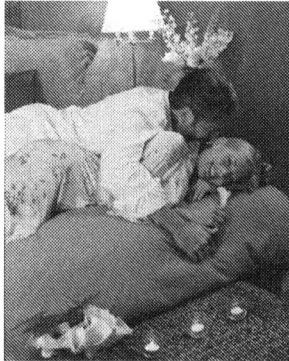

Three old women are sitting on a park bench when a man comes by and flashes them.

Two of them have a stroke… and the third one couldn't reach ☺

Mr. Smith goes to the doctor's office to collect his wife's test results.

Receptionist: "I'm sorry, sir, but there has been a bit of a mix-up and we have a problem. When we sent the samples from your wife to the lab, the samples from another Mrs. Smith were sent as well and we are now uncertain which one is your wife's. Frankly, that's either bad or terrible."

Mr. Smith: "What do you mean?"

Receptionist: "Well, one Mrs. Smith has tested positive for Alzheimer disease and the other was positive for AIDS. We can't tell which is your wife."

Mr. Smith: "That's terrible! Can we do the test over?"

Receptionist: "Normally, yes. But you have an HMO, and they won't pay for these expensive tests more than once."

Mr. Smith: "Well, what am I supposed to do now?"

Receptionist: "The doctor recommends that you drop your wife off in the middle of town. *If she finds her way home, don't sleep with her"* ☺

Three nuns were in the church discussing various rumors about the local priest. The first nun reported, "I was going through Father's office the other day, and do you know what I found? A bunch of pornographic magazines!"

The other nuns gasped. "What did you do?" they demanded. "Well, of course I threw them in the trash," she replied.

The second nun said, "Well, I can top that. I was in the Father's room putting away the laundry, and I found a bunch of condoms!

"Oh my!" gasped the other nuns, stunned at this apparent violation of the priest's chastity vow. "What did you do???" they asked. "I decided to teach him a lesson," said the second nun. "I poked holes in all of the condoms!"

The third nun fainted ☺

A Jewish grandmother is watching her grandchild playing on the beach when a huge wave comes and takes him out to sea.
She pleads, "Please G-d, save my only grandson. I beg of you, bring him back."
And a big wave comes and washes the boy back onto the beach, good as new. She looks up to heaven and says:
"He had a hat!" ☺

(Myron Cohen)

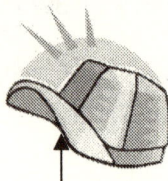

I knew these Siamese twins. They moved to England,
so the other one could drive ☺

(Steven Wright)

Two campers are walking through the woods when a huge brown bear suddenly appears in the clearing about 50 feet in front of them. The bear sees the campers and begins to head toward them.

The first guy drops his backpack, digs out a pair of sneakers, and frantically begins to put them on.

The second guy says "What are you doing? Sneakers won't help you outrun that bear."

"I don't need to outrun the bear," the first guy says.

"I just need to outrun you" ☺

 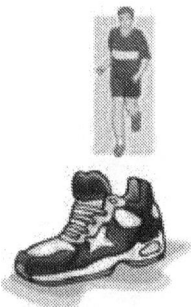

Why does Snoop Dogg always carry an umbrella?

Fo Drizzle! ☺

A guy has a talking dog. He brings it to a talent scout.
"This dog can speak English," he claims to the unimpressed agent. "Okay, Sport," the guys says to the dog, "what's on the top of a house?" "Roof!" the dog replies.
"Oh, come on..." the talent agent responds. "All dogs go 'roof'."
"No, wait," the guy says. He asks the dog "what does sandpaper feel like?" "Rough!" the dog answers.
The talent agent gives a condescending blank stare. He is losing his patience. "No, hang on," the guy says. "This one will amaze you. " He turns and asks the dog: "Who, in your opinion, was the greatest baseball player of all time?" "Ruth!" goes the dog.
And the talent scout, having seen enough, boots them out of his office onto the street. And the dog turns to the guy and says *"Maybe I shoulda said DiMaggio?"* ☺

I was so ugly when I was born, *the doctor slapped my mother* ☺
(Henny Youngman)

Three old men were talking about how much their hands shook.

The first old guy said, "My hands shake so bad, that when I shaved his morning, I cut my face."

The second old fogey one-upped him and said, "My hands shake so bad, that when I trimmed my garden yesterday, I sliced all my flowers."

The third old man laughed and said, "That's nothing. My hands shake so bad that when I took a piss yesterday, *I came three times!"* ☺

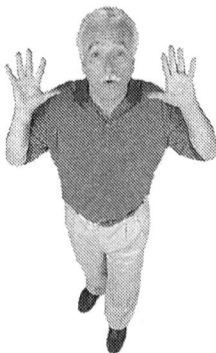

Why is President Clinton so reluctant to decide the fate of Elian Gonzalez?

Because last time he made a decision about where to put a Cuban he was almost impeached ☺

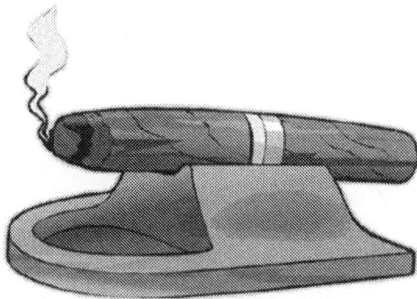

A guy has a parrot that can sing and speak beautifully. He takes it to the synagogue on Rosh Hashonah and makes a wager that the bird can conduct the High Holiday service better than the temple's cantor.

When the big moment comes, though, the parrot is silent. The guy is outraged. He takes the bird home and is about to kill it when the bird finally speaks:

"Schmuck! Think of the odds we'll get on Yom Kippur!" ☺

Rosh ✡ Hashanah

YOM ✡ KIPPUR

A Jewish guy goes into a confession box.

"Father O'Malley," he says, "my name is Emil Cohen.
I'm seventy-eight years old. Believe it or not, I'm currently involved with a 28 year old girl, and also, on the side, her 19 year old sister.
We engage in all manner of pleasure, and in my entire life I've never felt better."

"My good man," says the priest, "I think you've come to the wrong place. Why are you telling me?"

And the guy goes:
"I'm telling everybody!" ☺

A lawyer dies and goes to Heaven.
"There must be some mistake," the lawyer argues.
 "I'm too young to die. I'm only fifty five."
"Fifty five?" says Saint Peter.
 "No, according to out calculations, you're eighty two."
"How's you get that?" the lawyer asks.
St. Peter answers: "We added up your time sheets" ☺

I went to the psychiatrist, and he says
"You're crazy " I tell him I want a second opinion.
He says, 'Okay, you're ugly too!" ☺
(Rodney Dangerfield)

Mario Andretti has retired from race car driving. That's a good thing. He's getting old.

He ran his entire last race with his left blinker on ☺
(Jon Stewart)

A guy is sitting at home when he hears a knock at the door.

He opens the door and sees a snail on the porch.

He picks up the snail and throws it as far as he can.

Three years later, there's a knock on the door. He opens it and sees the same snail.
The snail says *'What the hell was that all about?"* ☺

I was making love to this girl and she started crying.
I said, "Are you going to hate yourself in the morning?"
She said. *"No. I hate myself now"* ☺
(Rodney Dangerfield)

Man goes into a cocktail lounge and approaches a woman sitting by herself:

Man: "May I buy you a cocktail?"

Lady: "No thank you, alcohol is bad for my legs."

Man: "Sorry to hear that. Do they swell?"

Lady: *"No, they open!"* ☺

Moses, Jesus, and an old, bearded man were out playing golf. Moses stepped up to the tee and drove a long one. It landed in the fairway but rolled directly toward the water. Quickly Moses raised his club, the water parted and it rolled to the other side safe and sound.

Next, Jesus strolls up to the tee and hits a nice long one directly toward the same water. It landed directly in the center of the pond and kind of hovered over the water. Jesus casually walked out on the pond and chipped it up onto the green.

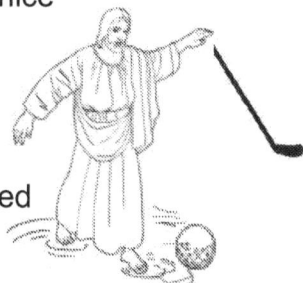

The third guy gets up and sort of randomly whacks the ball. It heads out over the fence and into oncoming traffic on a nearby street. It bounces off a truck and hits a nearby tree. From there it bounces onto the roof of a nearby shack and rolls down into the gutter, down the downspout, out onto the fairway and right toward the aforementioned pond. On the way to the pond, it hits a little stone and bounces out over the water and onto a lily pad where it rested quietly. Suddenly, a very large bullfrog jumped upon the lily pad and snatched the ball into his mouth. Just then, an eagle swooped down and grabbed the frog and flew away. As they passed over the green, the frog squealed with fright and Dropped the ball, which bounced right into the hole for a beautiful hole in one. Moses then turned to Jesus and said, *"I hate playing with your Dad"* ☺

Working people frequently ask retired people what they do to make their days interesting.

Well, for example, the other day I went into town and went into a shop. I was only in there for about 5 minutes, when I came out there was a cop writing out a parking ticket.

I went up to him and said, "Come on man, how about giving a senior citizen a break?" He ignored me and continued writing the ticket.

I called him a turd. He glared at me and started writing another ticket for having worn tires.

So I called him a ----head. He finished the second ticket and put it on the windshield with the first. Then he started writing a third ticket. This went on for about 20 minutes.

The more I abused him, the more tickets he wrote. Personally, I didn't care. I came into town by bus. I try to have a little fun each day now that I'm retired.

It's important at my age ☺

A group of girlfriends are on vacation, when they see a 5-story hotel with a sign that reads, "For Women Only". Since they were without their boyfriends or parents, they decide to go in.

The desk clerk, a very attractive guy, explains to them how it works. "We have 5 floors...go up floor by floor, and once you find what you are looking for, you can stay there. It's easy to decide, since each floor has signs telling you what's inside."

So they start going up, and on the first floor the sign reads, "All the men here have it short and thin." The friends laugh and without hesitation move on to the next floor.

The sign on the second floor reads, "All the men here have it long and thin."

Still, this wasn't good enough, so the friends move up to the third floor, where the sign reads, "All the men here have it short and thick." This was still another disappointment, but knowing there are still 2 floors left, they move on to the next floor.

On the fourth floor, the sign was perfect. "All the men here have it long and thick."

The women get all excited and are just about to go in when they realize that there is one floor left. Wondering what they were missing, they go to the fifth floor, where the sign reads,

"There are no men here. *This floor was built only to prove that there is no way to please a woman"* ☺

A farmer was worried that none of his pigs were getting pregnant. He called a vet and asked what he should do if he wanted more pigs. The vet told him he should try artificial insemination. The farmer, not wanting to appear stupid, answered okay and hung up the phone. Unclear on what the vet meant by artificial insemination, the farmer decided it must mean he had to impregnate the pigs himself, so he loaded all the pigs in his pickup, drove down to the woods, and shagged them all.

The next day he called the vet again, and asked how he would know if the pigs were pregnant. The vet told him they would be lying down rolling in the mud, but when he looked not even one was lying down. So he loaded them up in his pickup again, drove them to the woods, and shagged them all again.

To his dismay they were all standing the next morning. So, again he loads the pigs in his truck, drives them to the woods and shags them for the third time.

By the next morning the farmer is beat, so he asks his wife to hop out of bed and look out the window to see what the pigs are doing.

She says, "Hmmm - that's weird, they are all in the truck and one of them is blowing the horn" ☺

A Greek and an Italian were sitting in a St-rbucks one day discussing who had the superior culture.

Over triple lattes the Greek guy says, "We have the Parthenon."

Arching his eyebrows the Italian replies, "Well, we have the Coliseum."

The Greek retorts, "We Greeks gave birth to advanced mathematics."

The Italian, nodding in agreement, says, "But we built the Roman Empire."

And so on and so on until the Greek comes up with what he thinks will end the discussion. With a flourish of finality he says, "We invented sex!"

The Italian replies, *"That's true, but it was the Italians who introduced it to women"* ☺

---

3 brothers named Bu, Chu and Fu migrated to USA from China.

They decided to change their names:

Bu became Buck

Chu became Chuck.

Fu decided to go back to China ☺

Kenny the rooster cost a lot of money, but the farmer decides he'd be worth it. So, he buys Kenny.

The farmer takes Kenny home and sets him down in the barnyard, first, giving the rooster a pep talk. "I want you to pace yourself now. You've got a lot of chickens to service here, and you cost me a lot of money. Consequently, I'll need you to do a good job. So, take your time and have some fun," the farmer said, with a chuckle.

Kenny seemed to understand, so the farmer pointed toward the Hen house and Kenny took off like a shot. WHAM!- Kenny nails every hen in the hen house- three or four times, and the farmer is really shocked.

After that the farmer hears a commotion in the duck pen, sure enough, Kenny is in there.

Later, the farmer sees Kenny after a flock of geese, down by the lake. Once again - WHAM! He gets all the geese.

By sunset he sees Kenny out in the fields chasing quail and pheasants. The farmer is distraught and worried that his expensive rooster won't even last 24 hours. Sure enough, the farmer goes to bed and wakes up the next day, to find Kenny on his back, stone cold in the middle of the yard, vultures are circling overhead.

The farmer, saddened by the loss of such a colorful and expensive animal, shakes his head and says, "Oh, Kenny, I told you to pace yourself. I tried to get you to slow down, now look what you've done to yourself."

Kenny opens one eye, nods toward the vultures circling in the sky and says, *"Shhh, they're getting closer"* ☺

This guy was lonely and so he decided life would be more fun if he had a pet.

So he went to the pet store and told the owner that he wanted to buy an unusual pet. After some discussion, he finally bought a centipede, which came in a little white box to use for his house.

He took the box back home, found a good location for the box, and decided he would start off by taking his new pet to the bar to have a drink. So he asked the centipede in the box, "Would you like to go to Franks with me and have a beer?"

But there was no answer from his new pet. This bothered him a bit, but he waited a few minutes and then asked him again, "How about going to the bar and having a drink with me?" But again, there was no answer from his new friend and pet.

So he waited a few minutes more, thinking about the situation. He then decided to ask him one more time; this time putting his face up against the centipede's house and shouting, "Hey, in there! Would you like to go to Frank's place and have a drink with me?

A little voice came out of the box: "I heard you the first time! I'm putting my f-cking shoes on" ☺

A teacher asked her class, "What do you want out of life?"

A little girl in the back row raised her hand and said, "All I want out of life is four little animals!"

The teacher asked, "Really and what four little animals would that be?"

The little girl said, "A mink on my back, a jaguar in the garage, a tiger in the bed, and a jackass to pay for it all" ☺

"Doctor", the worried executive told the psychiatrist, "I'm afraid I'm schizophrenic"

"Well," the doctor replied, *"that makes four of us"* ☺

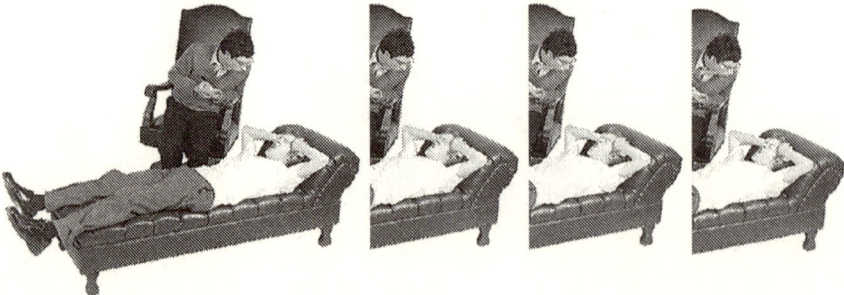

A truck driver hauling a tractor-trailer load of computers stops for a beer. As he approaches the bar he sees a big sign on the door saying: "NERDS NOT ALLOWED -- ENTER AT YOUR OWN RISK"

He goes in and sits down. The bartender comes over to him, sniffs, says he smells kind of nerdy, and asks him what he does for a living. The truck driver says he drives a truck, and the smell is just from the computers he is hauling. The bartender says OK, truck drivers are not nerds, and serves him a beer. As he is sipping his beer, a skinny guy walks in with tape around his glasses, a pocket protector with twelve kinds of pens and pencils stashed in his pocket protector, and a belt at least a foot too long. The bartender, without saying a word, pulls out a shotgun and blows the guy away. The truck driver asks him why he did that. The bartender said not to worry, "The nerds are overpopulating the Silicon Valley, and are in season now. You don't even need a license", he said.

So the truck driver finishes his beer, gets back in his truck, and heads back onto the freeway. Suddenly, he veers to avoid an accident and the load shifts. The back door breaks open and computers spill out all over the freeway. He jumps out and sees a crowd already forming, grabbing up the computers. They are all engineers, accountants, and programmers wearing the nerdiest clothes he has ever seen. He can't let them steal his whole load. So remembering what happened in the bar, he pulls out his gun and starts blasting away, felling several of them instantly.

A highway patrol officer comes zooming up and jumps out of the car screaming at him to stop. The truck driver says, "What's wrong? I thought nerds were in season."

"Well, sure," said the patrolman, "But you can't bait em" ☺

Two college students, Frank and Matt, are riding on a New York City subway when a beggar approaches them asking for spare change. Frank adamantly rejects the man in disgust. Matt, on the other hand, whips out his wallet, pulls out a couple of singles and gladly hands them over to the beggar with a smile.

The beggar thanks him kindly and then continues on to the other passengers. Frank is outraged by his friend's act of generosity.

"What on earth did you do that for?" shouts Frank. "You know he's only going to use it on drugs or booze."

Matt replies, "And we weren't?" ☺

Matt's dad picked him up from school to take him to a dental appointment. Knowing the parts for the school play were supposed to be posted that day, he asked his son if he got one.

Matt enthusiastically announced that he had. "I play a man who's been married for twenty years."

"That's great, son. Keep up the good work and before you know it they'll be giving you a speaking part" ☺

A lady walks into a bar, and sees a really good-looking guy sitting at the bar by himself. She goes over and asks him what he is drinking.

"Magic Beer," he says.

She thinks he's a little crazy, so she walks around the bar, but after realizing that there is no one else worth talking to, goes back to the man sitting at the bar and says, "That isn't really Magic Beer, is it?"

"Yes, I'll show you."

He takes a drink of the beer, jumps out the window, flies around the building three times and comes back in the window.

The lady can't believe it: "I bet you can't do that again."

He takes another drink of beer, jumps out the window, flies around the building three times, and comes back in the window.

She is so amazed that she says she wants a Magic Beer, so the guy says to the bartender, "Give her one of what I'm having."

She gets her drink, takes a gulp of the beer, jumps out the window, plummets 30 stories, breaks every bone in her body, and dies.

The bartender looks up at the guy and says, *"You know, Superman, you're a real asshole when you're drunk!!!"* ☺

A husband and wife were out golfing together one day when they came upon a tough par 4 hole. The husband hooked his drive deep into the woods and proclaimed that he would have to chip out. Then the wife said, "Maybe not, dear! Do you see that barn over there? If I open the doors on both sides, I do believe you could hit it right through and reach the green."

So the husband agrees to give it a try, but when he hits the ball it goes straight through the front doors of the barn, hits the crossbeam, ricochets back and hits his wife square in the head, killing her.

A year goes by and the man is golfing with a friend. He finds himself on the same hole, with the same results, a hook deep in the woods. He is all set to chip out when his friend runs up to him and says, "Wait! Do you see that barn over there? If I open the doors on both sides, I think you can still reach the green."

"No way," replies the man, *"I tried that last year and got a 7"* ☺

Over breakfast one morning, a woman said to her husband, "I bet you don't know what day this is." "Of course I do," he indignantly answered, going out the door to the office.

At 10 AM, the doorbell rang and when the woman opened the door, she was handed a box containing a dozen long stemmed red roses. At 1 PM, a foil wrapped, two-pound box of her favorite chocolates arrived. Later, a boutique delivered a designer dress.

The woman couldn't wait for her husband to come home. When he arrived, she exclaimed, "First the flowers, then the chocolates and then the dress!.

I've never had a more wonderful Groundhog Day in my life!" ☺

What's six inches long and two inches wide and drives women wild?

Money ☺

A young monk arrives at the monastery.

He is assigned to helping the other monks in copying the old canons and laws of the church by hand. He notices, however, that all of the monks are copying from copies, not from the original manuscript.

So, the new monk goes to the head abbot to question his, pointing out that if someone made even a small error in the first copy, it would never be picked up. In fact, that error would be continued in all of the subsequent copies. The head monk, says, "We have been copying from the copies for centuries, but you make a good point, my son." So, he goes down into the dark caves underneath the monastery where the original manuscripts are held as archives in a locked vault that hasn't been opened for hundreds of years.

Hours go by and nobody sees the old abbot. So, the young monk gets worried and goes down to look for him. He sees him banging his head against the wall and wailing, "We missed the "R", we missed the "R". His forehead is all bruised and he is crying uncontrollably. The young monk asks the old abbot, "What's wrong, father?" With a choking voice, the old abbot replies,

"The word was 'celebrate'" ☺

A bartender was working the late shift. While he was working, a beautiful blonde woman walked in and took a seat. She ordered up a Coors and sat there drinking it for a while. Suddenly, the woman passed out cold on the stool. The bartender had a sudden thought, and so he cautiously looked around. Seeing that no one was around, he closed up the bar, and took advantage of the situation.

The next night, the bartender was again working the late shift, but some of his friends stopped by, so he told them about the previous night and his good time with the blonde woman. All of a sudden, the blonde walks in again. The bartender motions to his friends that she is the same lady. The lady sits down at the bar and orders another Coors. Eventually, she passes out. The bartender closes up shop, and him and all of his friends take turns.

The next night, the bartender is working the late shift. His friends show up, with all of their friends, and so there is a huge crowd in the bar. The woman walks in again, orders a Coors, drinks it, and then passes out. So, the bartender closes up shop, and everyone has a turn.

The next night, even more people are waiting at the bar. The woman walks in and orders a Budweiser.

The bartender, his plans foiled, asks, "You don't want the usual?"
She looks at him and shakes her head.

"No. Coors makes my p-ssy sore" ☺

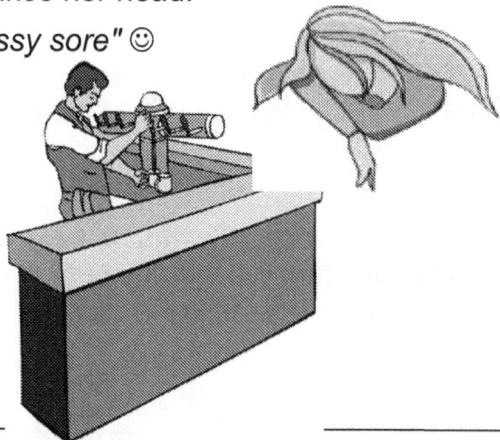

A mortician was working late one night.
He examined the body of Mr. Schwartz, about to be cremated, and made a startling discovery. Schwartz had the largest private part he had ever seen!
"I'm sorry Mr. Schwartz," the mortician commented, "I can't allow you to be cremated with such an impressive private part. It must be saved for posterity."
So, he removed it, stuffed it into his briefcase, and took it home.
"I have something to show you won't believe," he said to his wife, opening his briefcase.

"My G-d!" the wife exclaimed, "Schwartz is dead!" ☺

A woman was in bed with her lover when she heard her husband opening the front door. "Hurry," she said, "stand in the corner."
She rubbed baby oil all over him, then dusted him with talcum powder. "Don't move until I tell you," she said, " pretend you're a statue."

"What's this?" the husband inquired as he entered the room.
"Oh it's a statue," she replied, "the Smiths bought one and I liked it so I got one for us, too."

No more was said, not even when they went to bed. Around 2 AM the husband got up, went to the kitchen and returned with a sandwich and a beer.

"Here," he said to the statue, have this.
I stood like that for two days at the Smiths
and nobody offered me a damned thing" ☺

An 80-year old man goes to the doctor for a check-up. The doctor is amazed at what good shape the guy is in and asks, "How do you stay in such great physical condition?"

I'm a golfer," says the old guy, "and that's why I'm in such good shape. I play every day, including this morning."

"Well," says the doctor, "I'm sure that helps, but there's got to be more to it. How old was your dad when he died?"

My dad's still alive and 100 years old, he's a golfer too. He couldn't go golfing this morning because he's getting married today."

"Getting married!! Why would a 100 year-old guy want to get married?"

"Who said he wanted to?" ☺

Three little ducks go into a Bar.............................

"Say, what's your name?" the bartender asked the first duck.
"Huey," was the reply.
"How's your day been, Huey?"
"Great. Lovely day. Had a ball. Been in and out of puddles all day. What else could a duck want?" said Huey.
"Oh. That's nice," said the bartender. He turned to the second duck, "Hi, and what's your name?"
"Dewey," came the answer from duck number two.
"So how's your day been, Dewey?" he asked.
"Great. Lovely day. I've had a ball too. Been in and out of puddles all day myself. What else could a duck want?"
The bartender turned to the third duck and said, "So, you must be Louie?" "No," she said, batting her eyelashes.

"My name is Puddles" ☺

A man and his wife were sitting
in the living room and he said to her
"Just so you know, I never want to
live in a vegetative state, dependent
on some machine and fluids from
a bottle. If that ever happens,
just pull the plug."

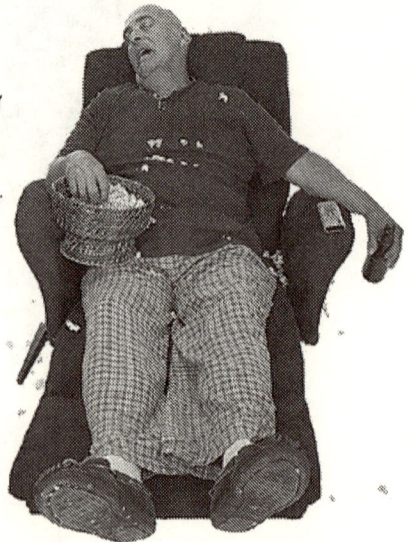

His wife got up, unplugged the TV and threw out all of his beer ☺

A married couple is driving down the interstate doing 55 mph. The husband is behind the wheel. His wife looks over at him and says, "Honey, I know we've been married for 15 years, but, I want a divorce."

The husband says nothing but slowly increases speed to 60 mph.

She then says, "I don't want you to try to talk me out of it, because I've been having an affair with your best friend, and he's a better lover than you."

Again the husband stays quiet and just speeds up as he clenches his hands on the wheels.

She says, "I want the house." Again the husband speeds up, and now is doing 70 mph.

She says, "I want the kids too." The husband just keeps driving faster, and faster, until he's up to 80 mph.

She says, "I want the car, the checking account, and all the credit cards too." The husband slowly starts to veer toward a bridge overpass piling, as she says, "Is there anything you want?"

The husband says, "No, I've got everything I need right here."

She asks, "What's that?"

The husband replies just before they hit the wall at 90 mph, "I've got the airbag!" ☺

Two aliens landed on a farm. The farmer and his wife took the aliens in and showed them their way of life and everything. One day the farmer and his wife get to talking. The farmer asks his wife, "I wonder what the aliens do for sex?" The farmer's wife replied, "I don't know. Do you want to find out?" The farmer agrees.

So, that night, the farmer took the female alien up to one room while his wife took the male alien up to another room. As the wife was getting into bed, she looked down at the alien's pecker and starts laughing. "You've got to be kidding me!" she laughed.

The alien told her to wait for a moment. Then he slapped his cheeks and pulled his ears and the thing grew. The next day, the farmer asks his wife, "So, how was your night?" She replied, "Oh, it was wonderful. It was the best night of my life! How was yours?"

"Well, not so good," replied the farmer, "all she kept doing all night was slapping my cheeks and pulling my ears" ☺

A farm boy accidentally overturned his wagonload of wheat on the road. The farmer that lived nearby came to investigate. "Hey, Willis," he called out, "forget your troubles for a while and come and have dinner with us. Then I'll help you overturn the wagon."

"That's very nice of you," Willis answered, "but I don't think Dad would like me to."

"Aw, come on, son!" the farmer insisted.

"Well, OK," the boy finally agreed, "but Dad won't like it."

After a hearty dinner, Willis thanked the host. "I feel a lot better now, but I know Dad's going to be real upset."

"Don't be silly!" said the neighbor. "By the way, where is he?"

"Under the wagon,"
replied Willis ☺

What's the difference between a lawyer and a bucket of shit?
The bucket! ☺

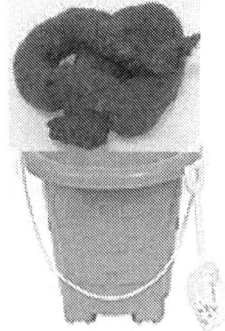

A young man goes into a drug store to buy condoms.

The pharmacist says the condoms come in packs of 3, 9 or 12 and asks which the young man wants. "Well," he said, "I've been seeing this girl for a while and she's really hot. I want the condoms because I think tonight's "the" night. We're having dinner with her parents, and then we're going out. And I've got a feeling I'm gonna get lucky after that. Once she's had me, she'll want me all the time, so you'd better give me the 12 pack." The young man makes his purchase and leaves.

Later that evening, he sits down to dinner with his girlfriend and her parents. He asks if he might give the blessing, and they agree. He begins the prayer, but continues praying for several minutes. The girl leans over and says, "You never told me that you were such a religious person."

He leans over to her and says,

"You never told me that your father is a pharmacist" ☺

What's the difference between a dead skunk in the road and a dead lawyer in the road?

There are skid marks in front of the skunk ☺

A man and wife were taking a shower when the doorbell rang. The wife says, "I'll get it" and wraps a towel around her. She opens the door and sees that it's her next door neighbor. The neighbor notices that she's in her towel and says, "Damn your fine! I'll give you $500 right now if you'll open your towel and let me get a good look at that beautiful body of yours"

She says, "$500? Right now?" He says, "Yeah right now." She agrees and opens her towel and lets him get a real good look. He hands her the $500 and goes back home. She gets back in the shower and her husband asks who was at the door and she says that it was the next door neighbor.

He said, "Cool! Did he have my 500 bucks?" ☺

A sweet grandmother telephoned Mount Sinai Hospital.
She timidly asked, "Is it possible to speak to some one who can tell me how a patient is doing?"

The operator said "I'll be glad to help, Dear..What's the name and room number?" The grandmother in her weak tremulous voice said, "Holly Finkel, room 302."

The Operator replied, "Let me check."

"Oh, good news. Her record says that Holly is doing very well. Her blood pressure is fine; her blood work just came back as normal and her physician, Dr. Cohen, has scheduled her to be discharged Tuesday."

The Grandmother said, "Thank you. That's wonderful! I was so worried! G-d bless you for the good news."

The operator replied, "You're more than welcome. Is Holly your daughter?"

The Grandmother said, "No, I'm Holly Finkel in 302. No one tells me shit" ☺

The madam opened the brothel door to see a rather dignified, well-dressed good-looking man in his late 40s or early 50s. "May I help you?" she asked. "I want to see Natalie," the man replied.

"Sir, Natalie is one of our most expensive ladies. Perhaps you would prefer someone else," said the madam. "No. I must see Natalie," was the man's reply.

Just then, Natalie appeared and announced to the man that she charged $1,000 a visit. Without hesitation, the man pulled out ten 100-dollar bills, gave them to Natalie, and they went upstairs. After an hour, the man calmly left.

The next night, the same man appeared again, demanding to see Natalie. Natalie explained that no one had ever come back two nights in a row--too expensive--and there were no discounts. The price was still $1,000. Again the man pulled out the money, gave it to Natalie and they went upstairs. After an hour, he left.

The following night the man was there again. Everyone was astounded that he had come for the third consecutive night, but he paid Natalie and they went upstairs. After their session, Natalie questioned the man. "No one has ever used me three nights in a row. Where are you from?" she asked.

The man replied, "South Carolina." "Really" she said. "I have family in South Carolina." "I know," the man said. "Your father died and I am your sister's attorney. *She asked me to give you your $3,000 inheritance"* ☺

The moral of the story is that three things in life are certain:
1. Death
2. Taxes
3. Being screwed by a lawyer

A man and a woman are riding next to each other in first class. The man sneezes, pulls out his wang and wipes the tip off. The woman can't believe what she just saw and decides she is hallucinating.

A few minutes pass. The man sneezes again. He pulls out his wang and wipes the tip off. The woman is about to go nuts. She can't believe that such a rude person exists. A few minutes pass. The man sneezes yet again. He takes his wang out and wipes the tip off. The woman has finally had enough. She turns to the man and says, "Three times you've sneezed, and three times you've removed your penis from your pants to wipe it off! What the hell kind of degenerate are you?"

The man replies, "I am sorry to have disturbed you, ma'am. I have a very rare condition such that when I sneeze, I have an orgasm."

The woman then says, "Oh, how strange. What are you taking for it?"

The man looks at her and says, "Pepper" ☺

A train hits a busload of catholic schoolgirls and they all perish. They all wind up in Heaven trying to enter the pearly gates past St. Peter.

St. Peter asks the first girl, "Karen, have you ever had any contact with a penis?" She giggles and shyly replies, "Well I once touched the head of one with the tip of my finger." St. Peter says, "OK, dip the tip of your finger in The Holy Water and pass through the gate."

St. Peter asks the next girl the same question, "Karina have you ever had any contact with a penis?" The girl is a little reluctant but replies, "Well once I fondled and stroked one." St. Peter says "OK, dip your whole hand in The Holy Water and pass through the gate."

All of a sudden there is a lot of commotion in the line of girls, one girl is pushing her way to the front of the line. When she reaches the front of the line St. Peter says "Sharon! What seems to be the rush?" *The girl replies "If I'm going to have to gargle that Holy Water, I want to do it before Mandy sticks her ass in it!"* ☺

A group of 3rd, 4th and 5th graders, accompanied by two female teachers, went on a field trip to the local racetrack to learn about thoroughbred horses and the supporting industry, but mostly to see the horses.

When it was time to take the children to the bathroom it was decided that the girls would go with one teacher and the boys would go with the other.

The teacher assigned to the boys was waiting outside the men's room when one of the boys came out and told her that none of them could reach the urinal.

As she lifted one, she couldn't help but notice that he was unusually well endowed. Trying not to show that she was staring, the teacher said, "You must be in the 5th grade."

No, ma'am, " he replied. "I'm the jockey riding Silver Arrow in the seventh ☺

Did you hear about the circumcision doctor who kept the foreskins and made himself a wallet?

When he rubbed the wallet, it turned into a briefcase! ☺

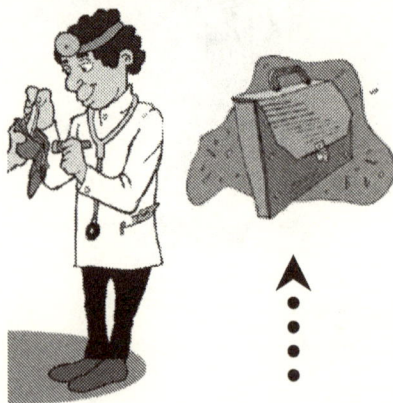

A guy goes to the local Post Office to apply for a job.

The interviewer asks him, "Have you been in the service?"

"Yes," he says. "I was in Viet Nam for three years."

The interviewer says, "That will give you extra points toward employment," and then asks, "Are you disabled in any way?"

The guy says, "Yes 100% ... a mortar round exploded near me and blew my testicles off."

The interviewer tells the guy, "O.K. I can hire you right now. The hours are from 8 a.m. to 4 p.m. You can start tomorrow. Come in at 10 a.m."

The guy is puzzled and says, "If the hours are from 8 a.m. to 4 p.m., then why do you want me to come in at 10 a.m.?"

"This is a government job" the interviewer explains. "For the first two hours we sit around scratching our balls...

No point in you coming in for that" ☺

A skinny little white guy goes into an elevator, looks up and sees this huge black guy standing next to him.

The big guy sees the little guy staring at him, looks down and says: "7 feet tall, 350 pounds, 20 inch private, 3 pound left testicle, 3 pound right testicle, Turner Brown."

The white man faints and falls to the floor. The big guy kneels down and brings him to, shaking him.

The big guy says, "What's wrong with you?"

In a weak voice the little guy says, "What EXACTLY did you say to me?"

The big dude says, "I saw the curious look and figured I'd just give you the answers to the questions everyone always asks me. I'm 7 feet tall, I weigh 350 pounds, I have a 20 inch private, my left testicle weighs 3 pounds, my right testicle weighs 3 pounds, and my name is Turner Brown."

The small guy says, "Turner Brown?!...
OH, Thank G-d! I thought you said turn around!" ☺

Last night they asked President Bush what he thought about Roe versus Wade.

He said, "I don't care how the people get out of New Orleans" ☺

Attending a wedding for the first time, a little girl whispered to her mother, "Why is the bride dressed in white?"

"Because white is the color of happiness, and today is the happiest day of her life."

The child thought about this for a moment, then said,

"So why is the groom wearing black?" ☺

Bill Clinton is sitting next to a 19-year-old White House intern one day at a gathering. The President says to her, "Would you like to come to the Oval Office and see my clock?"

She says, "No, Mr. President, I don't think so."

The President replies, "Please, I'd really like to show it to you."

"No, Mr. President, I really can't."

"Come on. Come and see my clock. It'll only take a minute."

"All right. If it won't take long.", replied the intern.

They go to the Oval Office. The President sits down, unzips his pants, and pulls out his penis.

The intern says, "Mr. President! That's not a clock, it's a cock!!!"

The President replies, "Well, you're right, but if you put two hands and a face on it, it's a clock" ☺

What's the difference between a tampon and a cowboy hat?

Cowboy hats are for assholes! ☺

When the ark's door was closed Noah called a meeting with all the animals.

"Listen up!" Noah said with a demanding voice. "There will be NO sex on this trip. All of you males take off your penis and hand it in to my sons.

I will sit over there and write you a receipt. After we see land, you can get your penis back."

After about a week Mr. Rabbit stormed into his wife's cage and was very excited. "Quick!" he said, "Get on my shoulders and look out the window to see if there is any land out there!" Mrs. Rabbit got onto his shoulders, looked out the window, and said, "Sorry, no land yet." "Damn!", exclaimed Mr. Rabbit.

This went on every day until Mrs. Rabbit got fed up with him. Mrs. Rabbit asked, "What is the matter with you? You know it will rain for forty days and nights. Only after the water has drained will we be able to see land. But why are you acting so excited every day?"

"Look!", said Mr. Rabbit with a sly expression, as he held out a piece of paper,

"I GOT THE HORSE'S RECEIPT!!" ☺

What do you call a musician who doesn't have a girlfriend?

Homeless! ☺

Why can't Helen Keller drive?

Because she's a woman ☺

What's 14 inches long
and hangs in front
of an asshole?

A lawyer's tie! ☺

Two guys are walking through the woods and come across this big hole. "Wow . . . that looks deep." "Sure does. . . toss a few pebbles in there and see how deep it is." They pick up a few pebbles and throw them in and wait . . . no noise "Man. That is REALLY deep . . . here . . . throw one of these great big rocks down there.

Those should make a noise." They pick up a couple football-sized rocks and toss them into the hole and wait . . and wait. Nothing.

They look at each other in amazement. One gets a determined look on his face and says, "Hey . . . over here in the weeds, there's a railroad tie. Help me carry it over here. When we toss that sucker in, it's GOTTA make some noise. The two drag the heavy tie over to the hole and heave it in. Not a sound comes from the hole.

Suddenly, out of the nearby woods, a goat appears, running like the wind. It rushes toward the two men, then right past them, running as fast as it's legs will carry it. Suddenly it leaps in the air and into the hole. The two men are astonished with what they've just seen . . . Then, out of the woods comes a farmer who spots the men and ambles over. "Hey . . . you two guys seen my goat out here?" "You bet we did! Craziest thing I ever seen! It came running like crazy and just jumped into this hole!" "Nah", say the farmer,

"That couldn't have been MY goat.

My goat was chained to a railroad tie ☺

A modern day cowboy has spent many days crossing the Texas plains without water. His horse has already died of thirst. He's crawling through the sand, certain that he has breathed his last breath, when all of a sudden he sees an object sticking out of the sand several yards ahead of him.

He crawls to the object, pulls it out of the sand, and discovers what looks to be an old briefcase. He opens it and out pops a genie. But this is no ordinary genie. She is wearing a FEMA ID badge and a dull gray dress. There's a calculator in her pocketbook. She has a pencil tucked behind one ear.
"Well, cowboy," says the genie... "You know how I work. You have three wishes."
"I'm not falling for this." said the cowboy. "I'm not going to trust a FEMA genie."
"What do you have to lose? You've got no transportation, and it looks like you're a goner anyway!"
The cowboy thinks about this for a minute, and decides that the genie is right. "OK, I wish I were in a lush oasis with plenty of food and drink."
POOF The cowboy finds himself in the most beautiful oasis he has ever seen, and he is surrounded with jugs of wine and platters of delicacies.
"OK, cowpoke, what's your second wish."

"My second wish is that I was rich beyond my wildest dreams."
POOF The cowboy finds himself surrounded by treasure chests filled with rare gold coins and precious gems.
"OK, cowpuncher, you have just one more wish. Better make it a good one!"
After thinking for a few minutes, the cowboy says... "I wish that no matter where I go, beautiful women will want and need me."

POOF *He turned into a tampon* ☺

The moral of the story: If the government offers you anything... there's going to be a string attached.

What's the difference between a porcupine and a BMW?

A porcupine has the pricks on the outside ☺

A Stanford Medical research group advertised for participants in a study of obsessive-compulsive disorder.

They were looking for therapy clients who had been diagnosed with this disorder.

The response was gratifying; they got 3,879 responses one hour after the ad came out.

All from the same person ☺

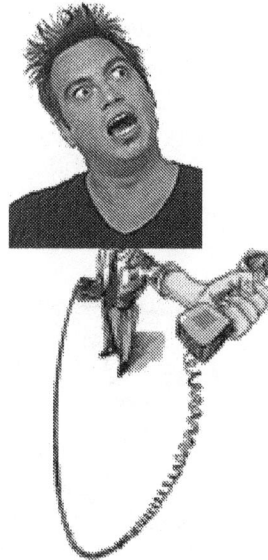

Two elderly women were out driving in a large car, both could barely see over the dashboard. As they were cruising along they came to an intersection. The stoplight was red but they just went on through.

The woman in the passenger seat thought to herself, "I must be losing my mind, I swear we just went through a red light."

After a few more minutes they came to another intersection and the light was red again, and again they went right through. This time the woman in the passenger seat was almost sure that the light had been red, but was really concerned that she was mistaken.

She was getting nervous and decided to pay very close attention to the road and the next intersection to see what was going on.

At the next intersection, sure enough, the light was definitely red and they went right through. She turned to woman driving and said, "Mildred! Did you know we just ran through three red lights in a row! You could have killed us!"

Mildred turned to her and said, "Oh, am I driving?" ☺

PART 4: <u>GREAT POLITICALLY INCORRECT JOKES!</u>

I have never been politically correct.

Most of my friends will tell you that I basically tell it as it is, without pulling any punches. As a result, most of my jokes fall in this section. I like 'em, and they work for me.

Tell whatever jokes that light you up, make 'em yours and own them! The more jokes that you tell the better joketeller you will be - I promise you that.

What's the first thing a girl from Tennessee says after she loses her virginity?

Get off me daddy, you're crushing my cigarettes ☺

Why did G-d create yeast infections?

*So women would know what it was like
to live with a miserable cunt* ☺

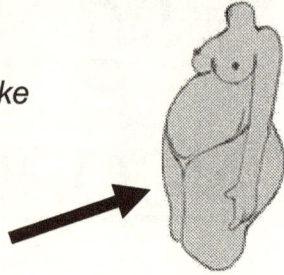

A guy dies and is sent to Hell.

Satan meets him, shows him doors to three rooms, and says he must choose one to spend eternity in.
In the first room, people are standing in shit up to their necks.
The guy says "no, let me see the next room."
In the second room, people are standing with shit up to their noses. Guy says no again.

Finally, Satan opens the door to the third room. People are standing with shit up to their knees, drinking coffee and eating danish pastries. The guy says, "I pick this room." Satan says okay and starts to leave, and the guy wades in and starts pouring some coffee.

On the way out Satan yells,

"O.K., coffee break's over. Everyone back on your heads!" ☺

A man is driving his five year old to a friend's house when another car races in front and cuts them off, nearly causing an accident. "Douchebag!" the father yells. A moment later he realizes the indiscretion, pulls over, and turns to face his son. "Your father just said a bad word," he says. "I was angry at that driver, but that was no excuse for what I said. It was wrong. But just because I said it, it doesn't make it right, and I don't ever want to hear you saying it. Is that clear?"

His son looks at him and says: "Too late, douchebag" ☺

Three kids come down to the kitchen and sit around the breakfast table. The mother asks the oldest boy what he'd like to eat. "I'll have some f-cking French toast," he says. The mother is outraged at his language, hits him, and sends him upstairs. She asks the middle child what he wants. "Well, I guess that leaves more f-cking French toast for me," he says. She is livid, smacks him, and sends him away. Finally she asks the youngest son what he wants for breakfast.

"I don't know," he says meekly, "but I definitely don't want the f-cking French toast" ☺

I was walking across a bridge one day, and I saw a man standing on the edge, about to jump off. So I ran over and said "Stop! Don't do it!" "Why shouldn't I?" he said.
"Well, there's so much to live for!"
"Like what?"
"Well... are you religious?"
He said yes.
I said, "Me too! Are you Christian or Buddhist?"
"Christian."
"Me too!
Are you Catholic or Protestant ?
"Protestant."
"Me too! Are you Episcopalian or Baptist?"
"Baptist"
"Wow! Me too! Are you Baptist Church of G-d or Baptist Church of the Lord?"
"Baptist Church of G-d!"
"Me too!
Are you original Baptist Church of G-d, or are you reformed Baptist Church of G-d?"
"Reformed Baptist Church of G-d!"
"Me too! Are you Reformed Baptist Church of G-d, reformation of 1879, or Reformed Baptist Church of G-d, reformation of 1915?"
He said, "Reformed Baptist Church of G-d, reformation of 1915!"

I said, "Die, heretic scum" and pushed him off (Emo Philips) ☺

How do you castrate a priest?

Kick the altar boy in the chin ☺

A Jewish man is walking on the beach when he discovers a bottle containing genie. He rubs it and a genie comes out, promises to grant him one wish.
He says, "Peace in the Middle east, that's my wish."

The genie looks concerned, then says "No, I'm sorry, that's just not possible. Some things just can't be changed. Do you have another wish?"

The guys says 'Well...for my whole life I've never received oral sex from my wife. That would be my wish."

The genie pauses for another moment and then says

"How would you define peace?" ☺

This guy runs home and bursts in yelling, "Pack your bags honey, I just won the lottery!"

She says, "Oh wonderful! Should I pack for the beach or the mountains?"

He replies, "I don't care...
Just get the f-ck out!" ☺

Why do women have legs?

So they don't leave trails like slugs ☺

These three women were sitting around one night talking about there boyfriends when they decided they would give their men nicknames based on kinds of soda.

The first woman said: "I'm gonna call Tom 'Mountain Dew' because he is as strong as a mountain and always wants to do it!"

The second woman said: "I'm gonna call Bruce '7-Up' because he has Seven inches and it is always up!"

The third woman said: "I'm gonna call my man 'Jack Daniels'."

The other two women responded: "Jack Daniels? But that's a hard liquor."

The third woman replied:

"THAT'S MY LEROY!" ☺

A man entered a restaurant and sat at the only open table. As he sat down, he knocked the spoon off the table with his elbow. A nearby waiter quickly reached into his shirt pocket, pulled out a clean spoon and set it on the table. The diner was very impressed.

"Do all the waiters carry spoons in their pockets?" he asked.

The waiter replied, "Yes. Ever since we had that efficiency expert out, he determined that 17.8% of our customers knock the spoon off the table. By carrying clean spoons with us, we save trips to the kitchen."

The man proceeded to finish his meal and went to pay the waiter. As he paid he commented "Forgive the intrusion, but do you know that you have a string hanging from your fly?

The waiter replied, "Yes, we all do. Seems that the same efficiency expert determined that we spend too much time washing our hands after using the men's room. So, the other end of that string is tied to my penis.

When I need to go, I simply pull the string, go to the bathroom, and return to work. Having never touched myself, there is no need to wash my hands. It is very efficient!"

"Wait a minute," queried the diner, "how do you get your penis back in your pants?"

"Well, I don't know about the other guys, but I use the spoon" ☺

Robert is a hard worker, and he spends most of his nights bowling or playing volleyball. One weekend, his wife decides that he needs to relax a little and take a break from sports, so she takes him to a strip club.

The doorman at the club spots them and says "Hey, Robert! How are you tonight?" His wife, surprised, asks her husband if he has been here before. "No, no, I can explain, He's just one of the guys I bowl with."

They are seated, and the waitress approaches, sees Robert and says, "Nice to see you, Robert. A Southern Comfort and Lemonade, as usual?". His wife's eyes widen. "You must come here a lot!" "No, no" says Robert, "I can explain, I just know her from volleyball".

Then a stripper walks up to the table. She throws her arms around Robert and says "Robert! A table dance as usual?"

His wife, fuming, collects her things and storms out of the bar. Robert follows her and spots her getting into a cab, so he jumps into the passenger seat. His wife looks at him, seething with fury and lets Robert have it with both barrels.

At this, the cabby leans over and says, "Sure looks like you picked up a wild one tonight, Robert!" ☺

One day when Bill Clinton and Al Gore were in Nashville, Al took Bill on a tour of his farm east of there. After a tour of the barn, they walked around behind it and discovered a sheep with it's head stuck in the fence.

As Bill watched the ewe struggle, he dropped his pants, fell to his knees and mounted the sheep. When he finished he turned to Al and said, "Why don't you try some of that?"

Al said, "Ok!" *and dropped his pants, fell to his knees and stuck his head in the fence* ☺

A woman is working late at a sperm bank. All of a sudden a man breaks through the window with a ski mask on and a gun in his hand. He looks at the woman and says,

"Drink one of the sperm samples or else I'll blow your brains out!!" The woman looks very disturbed and grabs a sample and drinks it down.

The man looks at her and puts his gun away, then he pulls his ski off

to reveal it is her husband. He says,

"See honey that wasn't so bad was it?" ☺

Little Johnny was 12 years-old and like other boys his age, rather curious he had been hearing quite a bit about "courting" from the older boys and he wondered what it was and how it was done. One day he took his questions to his mother who became rather flustered.

Instead of explaining "things" to Johnny she told him to hide behind the curtains one night and watch his older sister and her boyfriend. This he did. The following morning Johnny described everything he saw to his mother...

Sis and her boyfriend sat and talked for a while, then he turned off most of the lights. Then he started kissing and hugging her, I figured sis must be getting sick because her face started looking funny. He must have thought so too because he put his hand inside her blouse to feel her heart, just like the doctor would. Except he's not as smart as the doctor, because he seemed to have trouble finding her heart.

I guess he was getting sick too because pretty soon both of them started panting and getting all out of breath. His other hand must have been cold because he put it under her skirt. About this time sis got worse and began to moan and sigh and squirm around and slide down toward the end of the couch. This was when the fever started. I knew it was a fever because sis told
him she was really hot.

Finally, I found what was making them so sick - a big eel had gotten inside his pants somehow. It just jumped out of his pants and stood there, about ten inches long. Honest!! Anyway, he grabbed it in one hand to keep it from getting away.

When sis saw it, she got really scared, her eyes got big and her mouth fell open and she started calling to G-d and stuff like that. She said it was the biggest one she'd ever seen - I should tell her about the ones down at the lake.

Anyway, sis got brave and tried to kill the eel by biting its head off. All of a sudden she made a noise and let the eel go, I guess it bit her back. Then she grabbed it with both hands and held it tight while he took a muzzle out of his pocket and slipped it over the eel's head to keep it from biting again.

Sis laid back and spread her legs so she could get a scissor-lock on it and he helped her by laying on top of the eel. The eel put up a helluva fight. Sis started moaning and squealing and her boyfriend almost upset the couch. I guess they wanted to kill the eel.

After a while, they both quit moving and gave a great sigh. Her boyfriend got up and sure enough they had killed the eel. I knew it was dead because it just hung there limp, and some of its insides were hanging out.

Sis and her boyfriend were a little tired from the battle, but they went back to courting anyway. He started hugging and kissing her again. By golly, the eel wasn't dead!!! It jumped straight up and started to fight again, I guess that eel's are like cat's they have nine lives or something.

This time, sis jumped up and tried to kill the eel by sitting on it. After a 35 minute struggle they finally killed it again.

I knew it was dead this time because I saw sis's boyfriend peel its skin off and flush it down the toilet!! ☺

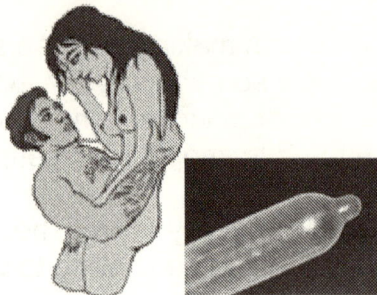

"Doctor," the embarrassed man said, "I have a sexual problem. I can't get it up for my wife anymore."

The Doctor looked at the man, and replied, "Mr. Thomas, bring her back with you tomorrow and let me see what I can do."

The next day the worried fellow returned with his wife. "Take off your clothes, Mrs. Thomas," the Doctor requested.
"Now turn all the way around...Lie down please...Uh- huh, I see. OK, you may put your clothes back on."

The doctor took the husband aside. "You're in perfect health," he said.

"Your wife didn't give me an erection either" ☺

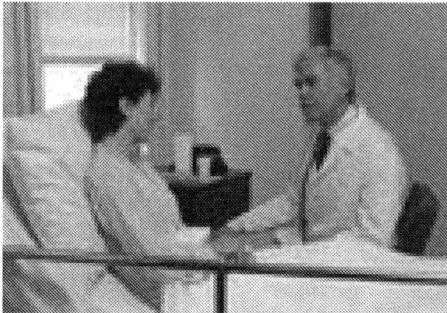

A housewife is at home when she suddenly hears a knock on the door. When she opens the door a man asks her if she has a vagina. The woman slams the door in disbelief at what a stranger has just asked her.

The same thing happens for three consecutive days and the woman decides to tell her husband.

The husband says to the wife, "Tomorrow I am not going to work, and when the man asks if you have a vagina, say 'yes' and I will be hiding behind the door."

The next day the same man comes again, and when the woman opens the door he asks if she has a vagina. The woman says, "Yes".

The man then said,

"Good, then please tell your husband to stop f-cking my wife" ☺

A chicken and an egg are lying in bed. The chicken is leaning against the headboard smoking a cigarette, with a satisfied smile on its face.

The egg, looking a bit pissed off, grabs the sheet, rolls over, and says,

"Well, I guess we finally answered THAT question" ☺

What is the difference between a ho and a bitch?

A ho will f-ck anybody, but a bitch will f-ck anybody but you! ☺

Little Johnny is passing his parent's bedroom in the middle of the night, in search of a glass of water. Hearing a lot of moaning and thumping, he peeks in and catches his folks screwing.

Before his dad can even react, Little Johnny exclaims, "Oh, boy! Horsie ride! Daddy, can I ride on your back?"

His dad, relieved that Johnny's not asking more uncomfortable questions, and seeing the opportunity not to break his stride, agrees. Johnny hops on and daddy starts going to town. Pretty soon mommy starts moaning and gasping.

Johnny cries out, "Hang on tight, Daddy!

This is the part where me and the milkman usually get bucked off!" ☺

An old couple is taking a trip down memory lane, and as such gone for a holiday back to the place where they first met. While sitting at a café the little old man says, "Remember the first time I met you over fifty years ago? We left this café, went round the corner behind the gas works and I gave you one from behind." "Why, yes I remember it well dear.", replies the little old lady with a grin.

"Well, for old time's sake, lets go back there and I'll give you one from behind again.", says the old man.

The couple pays their bill and leaves the café. A young man sitting next to them has overheard the conversation and smiles to himself, thinking it would be quite amusing to see the old couple go at it. He gets up and follows them.

Sure enough, he sees the couple near the gas works. The little old lady pulls off her knickers and lifts up her dress. The old man pulls down his pants and grabs the lady's hips. The little old lady then reaches for the fence. Well, what follows is forty minutes of the most athletic sex the man has ever seen. The little old man is banging away at the little old women at a pace that can only be described as phenomenal. Limbs are flying everywhere, the movement is a blur and they do not stop for a single second. Finally, they collapse and don't move for an hour.

Well, the man is stunned. Never in his life has he ever seen anything that equates to this, not in the movies, not from his friends or his own experiences. Reflecting on what he has just seen, he says to himself, "I have to know his secret. If only I could shag like that now, let alone in fifty years time!"

The two have by this time recovered and dressed themselves. Plucking up courage the man approaches the couple. He says, "Sir, in all my life I have never seen anybody shag like that, particularly at your age. What's your secret? Could you shag like that fifty years ago?"

The pensioner replies *"Son, fifty years ago that f-cking fence wasn't electrified"* ☺

What do Rice Krispies and Monica Lewinsky have in common?

They both talk after being hit with a white milky substance ☺

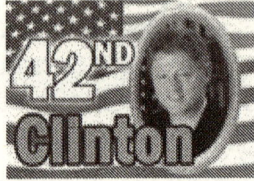

What do gay guys call hemorrhoids?

Speed bumps ☺

On a senior citizen bus tour, the driver was surprised.

While the passengers were unloading, to do some sightseeing, one elderly lady stopped and whispered in his ear, "Driver, I believe that I was sexually harassed!" The driver didn't think much of this complaint, but promised he would check into it soon.

Later, that very same day, as the passengers were unloading again, a second little old lady bent down and whispered in his ear, "Sir, I believe I was sexually harassed!" This time, he knew it had to be taken care of soon. A few passengers had remained on the bus, and he decided to go back and question them, to see if they had any knowledge of what was going on.

He found one little old man crawling along the bus floor underneath the seats and stooped down to question him. "Excuse me, sir, can I help you?" The elderly man looked up and said, "Well, sonny, you sure can. I've lost my toupee and I'm trying to find it.

I thought I'd located it twice, but they were parted in the middle, and mine's parted on the side!" ☺

Well there was this couple who had been married for 50 years. They were sitting at the breakfast table that morning when the old gentleman said to his wife, "Just think, honey, we've been married for 50 years."

"Yeah", she replied, "Just think, fifty years ago we were sitting here at this breakfast table together."

"I know", the old man said, "We were probably sitting here naked as jaybirds fifty years ago."

"Well", Granny snickered, "What do you say...should we?" Whereupon the two stripped to the buff and sat down at the table.

"You know, honey," the little old lady breathlessly replied, "My nipples are as hot for you as they were fifty years ago.

"I wouldn't be surprised", replied Gramps. "One's in your coffee and the other is in your oatmeal ☺

It's April 1st and a woman goes into labor. She is rushed to the hospital, gets drugged up, and the baby is delivered. When she wakes up she asks the doctor to see her baby. He brings it in drops it on the floor, kicks it across the room, picks it up, slaps it in the face, and throws it out the window.
At this, the woman starts to flip out screaming, "What are you doing!! That's my baby!!"
The doctor replies,

"April Fools!!! It was already dead!!" ☺

Two women are hiking in the woods. After an hour or so, they come to a stream. Unable to cross, they decide to walk along the stream and look for a narrower place.

Fortunately they come to an old bridge spanning the stream. Deciding the bridge safe, the two women proceed to cross. Halfway across, one woman stops and says to the other, "I've always wanted to be like the guys, and urinate off a bridge." The other woman looks around and says, "well, I don't see anyone around, now's your chance!" The first woman drops her hiking shorts and backs over to the side of the bridge.

As she begins to urinate, she looks over her shoulder. "Holy shit!" she exclaims, "I just pissed in a canoe!" Alarmed, the second woman hurries over, and peeks at the stream.

"Calm down," she says.

"That wasn't a canoe you pissed in, it was only your reflection"
☺

This couple had a wonderful relationship, or so the man thought until one day he came home from work to find his girlfriend packing.

He asked her why she was packing, and she replied that she had heard some horrible things about him.

He asked, "What could you have possibly heard about me to make you want to move out?"

"Someone told me that you were a pedophile."

He replied,

"That's an awfully big word for a ten year old" ☺

A married couple is driving along when they see a wounded skunk on the side of the road. They stop; the wife gets out, picks it up, and brings it into the car. She says, "Look, it's shivering, it must be cold. What should I do?" Her husband replies, "Put it between your legs to keep it warm." She asks, "What about the smell?"

He says,

"Hold its nose" ☺

A hippie gets onto a bus and proceeds to sit next to a nun in the front seat. The hippie looks over and asks the nun if she would have sex with him. The nun surprised by the question politely declines and gets off at the next stop.

When the bus starts on its way Bob the bus driver says to the hippie, "If you want, I can tell you how you can get that nun to have sex with you." The hippie says that he'd love to know, so the bus driver tells him that every Tuesday evening at midnight the nun goes to the cemetery to pray to the Lord. "If you went dressed in robes and some glowing powder," said the bus driver, "you could tell her you were G-d and command her to have sex with you." Well the hippie decides to try this out so that Tuesday he goes to the cemetery and waits for the nun. And right on schedule the nun shows up. When she's in the middle of praying the hippie walks out from hiding, in robes and glowing with a mask of G-d.

"I am G-d, I have heard your prayers and I will answer them but you must have sex with me first." The nun agrees but asks for anal sex so she might keep her virginity.

The hippie agrees to this and quickly sets about to go to work on the nun. After the hippie finishes, he rips off his mask and shouts out, "Ha ha, I'm the hippie!!"

The nun replied by whipping off her mask and shouting, "Ha ha, I'm the bus driver!!" ☺

One Sunday morning George burst into the living room and said, "Dad! Mom! I have some great news for you!

I am getting married to the most beautiful girl in town. She lives only a street away and her name is Susan Hoffman."

After dinner, George's dad took him aside and said, "Son, I have to talk with you. Look at your mother, George. She and I have been married 30 years, and she's a wonderful wife and mother, but she has never offered much excitement in the bedroom, so I fooled around with other women a lot. Susan Hoffman is actually your half sister, so I'm afraid you can't marry her." George was brokenhearted.

After eight months, he started dating girls again. A year later he came home and very proudly announced, "Diane said yes! We're getting married in June." Again his father insisted on another private conversation and broke the sad news: "Diane is your half sister too, George. I'm awfully sorry about this."

George was livid!

He finally decided to go to his mother with the news his father had shared. "Dad has done so much harm. I guess I'm never going to get married," he complained. "Every time I fall in love, Dad tells me the girl is my half sister." "Hah," his mother chuckled, shaking her head,

"Don't pay any attention to what he says. He's not really your father!" ☺

A little old lady with blue hair entered the sex aids shop and asked in a quavering voice, "Yy-young man, dd-do y-you sell-l d-dildos h-here?" The salesman, somewhat taken aback by the little old lady's appearance in his shop, answered, "Uh, yes ma'am. We do."

The little old lady, holding her quivering hands about 10 inches apart asked "D-do y-you ha-ave an-ny ab-bb-bout th-this lon-ong?" "Well, yes ma-am, we do. We have several that size."

Forming a 5" circle with her fingers, she then asked,"A-are an-nny of t-them about thi-is b-big ar-round-d?" "Well.... yes ma'am, a few of them are about that big."

"D-do aa-ny of t-them ha-ave a v-v-vibra-a-ator?"
"Yes ma'am, one of them does."

"W-w-ell, h-how d-do yo-ou t-turn it off?" ☺

Every day, a male co-worker walks up very close to a lady standing at the coffee machine, inhales a big breath of air and tells her that her hair smells nice.

After a week of this, she can't stand it anymore, takes her complaint to a supervisor of sexual harassment in the personnel department and states that she wants to write a grievance against him.

`The Human Resources supervisor is puzzled by this decision and asks, "What's sexually threatening about a co-worker telling you your hair smells nice?"

The woman replies,

"It's Keith, the midget" ☺

A man and a woman are sitting side by side at a bar getting really wasted. They are both really depressed.

The man asks the woman why she's so down and she replies, "My husband left me because he said I was too kinky in bed."

"What a coincidence!" he said, "My wife just left me. She said I was too kinky in bed too."

So they start talking and they find that they have much in common so they decide to go to the woman's apartment and have kinky sex.

When they arrive at her apartment, she tells him she needs a few minutes so she can slip into something more comfortable. She comes out of the bathroom with a tight, black leather outfit with a whip, handcuffs, a strap-on cock, and a 12 inch studded dildo. Then she hurries into the kitchen and comes out with tabasco sauce, whipped cream, and a rolling pin.

Then she notices that the man is putting on his coat and is walking towards the door.

"What's going on?" she asks. "I thought you wanted to get kinky?"

He turns around and says, "I just f-cked your dog and shit in your purse. I'm all done" ☺

Harold is 95 and lives in a senior citizen home. Every night after dinner, Harold goes to a secluded garden behind the center to sit and ponder his accomplishments and long life.

One evening, Mildred, age 87, wanders into the garden. They begin to chat, and before they know it, several hours have passed. After a short lull in their conversation, Harold turns to Mildred and asks, Do you know what I miss most of all?"

She asks, "What?" and he replies "SEX!!" Mildred exclaims, "Why you old fart you couldn't get it up if I held a gun to your head!"

"I know," Harold says, "but it would be nice if a woman could just hold it for a while." "Well, I can oblige," says Mildred, who unzips his trousers, removes his manhood and proceeds to hold it. Afterward, they agree to meet secretly each night in the garden where they would sit and talk and Mildred would hold Harold's manhood.

Then, one night, Harold didn't show up at their usual meeting place. Alarmed, Mildred decided to find Harold and make sure he was O.K.

She walked around the senior citizen home where she found him sitting by the pool with another female resident, Ethel, who was holding Harold's manhood!

Furious, Mildred yelled, "You two-timing creep! What does Ethel have that I don't have?"

Old Harold smiled happily and replied..............

"Parkinson's" ☺

A City cop was on his horse waiting to cross the street when a little girl on her new shiny bike stopped beside him.

"Nice bike", said the cop, "Did Santa bring it to you?"

"Yep," the little girl said, "He sure did!"

The cop looked the bike over and handed the girl a $5.00 ticket for a safety violation. The cop said, "Next year tell Santa to put a reflector light on the back of it."

The young girl looked up at the cop and said, "Nice horse you got there, sir, did Santa bring it to you?"

"Yes, he sure did," chuckled the cop.

The little girl looked up at the cop and said,

"Next year tell Santa the dick goes underneath the horse, not on top" ☺

A teenage girl came home from school and asks her mother, "Is it true what Rita just told me?"

"What's that?" asks her mother.

"That babies come out of the same place where boys put their penises?" said her daughter.

"Yes it is dear!" replies her mother, pleased that the subject had finally come up and that she wouldn't have to explain it to her daughter.

"But then, when I have a baby," responded the teenager, *"won't it knock my teeth out?"* ☺

A man from Utah has 20 wives, each of whom he makes love to every day. A New York City promoter hears of the man's daily regimen and hires him to exhibit his prowess on Broadway.

On opening night, the man from Utah makes love to only 10 of his wives before he collapses in exhaustion.

The curtain falls, and the promoter runs up to the man. "What happened?" the promoter asks.

"I don't know," the man answers.

"Everything went fine in rehearsal today" ☺

What is the difference between a condom and a coffin?

You come in one and you go in the other! ☺

A few months after his parents were divorced, little Johnny passed by his mom's bedroom and saw her rubbing her body and moaning, "I need a man, I need a man!"

Over the next couple of months, he saw her doing this several times.

One day, he came home from school and heard her moaning. When he peeked into her bedroom, he saw a man on top of her. Little Johnny ran into his room, took off his clothes, threw himself on his bed, started stroking himself, and moaning,

"Ohh, I need a bike! I need a bike!" ☺

What did the man lying on the beach say to Michael Jackson?

Get out of my son!!! ☺

A man traveling by plane and in urgent need to use the men's room is nervously tapping his foot on the floor of the aircraft. Each time he tried the men's room door, it was "OCCUPIED". The stewardess, aware of his predicament suggested that he go ahead and use the ladies room, but cautioned him against using any of the buttons inside.

The buttons were marked "WW, WA, PP and ATR".

Making the mistake that so many men make in disregarding the importance of what a woman says, the man let his curiosity get the best of him and decided to try the buttons anyway.

He carefully pressed the first button marked "WW" and immediately warm water sprayed all over his entire bottom. He thought, "WOW, the women really have it made!". Still curious, he pressed the button marked "WA" and a gentle breeze of warm air quickly dried his hind quarters.
He thought that was out of this world! The button marked "PP" yielded a large powder puff which delicately applied a soft talc to his rear. Well, naturally he couldn't resist the last button marked "ATR".

When he woke up in the hospital he panicked and buzzed for the nurse. When she appeared, he cried out, "What happened to me?! The last thing I remember is I was in the ladies room on a business trip!"

The nurse replied, "Yes, you were having a great time until you pressed the "ATR" button which stands for Automatic Tampon Remover...

Your penis is under your pillow!" ☺

A Navy Chief and an Admiral were sitting in the barbershop.

They were both just getting finished with their shaves. The barbers were reaching for some after-shave to slap on their faces. The admiral shouted, "Hey, don't put that stuff on me! My wife will think I've been in a whorehouse!"

The chief turned to his barber and said, "Go ahead and put it on.

My wife doesn't know what the inside of a whorehouse smells like" ☺

What's the difference between
a new husband and a new dog?

*After a year, the dog
is still excited to see you* ☺

Why is it so hard for women to find men that are sensitive, caring, and good looking?

Because those men already have boyfriends ☺

What makes men chase women they have no intention of marrying?

The same urge that makes dogs chase cars they have no intention of driving ☺

What is the quickest way to clear out a men's restroom?

Say, "Nice Dick" ☺

Why don't bunnies make noise when they have sex?

Because they have cotton balls ☺

What's the difference between a Northern fairytale and a Southern fairytale?

A Northern fairytale begins "Once upon a time." A Southern fairytale begins "'Y'all ain't gonna believe this...." ☺

How many women does it take to change a light bulb?

None, they just sit there in the dark and bitch ☺

Pinocchio had a human girlfriend who would sometimes complain about splinters when they were having sex. Pinocchico, therefore, went to visit Gepetto to see if he could help.

Gepetto suggested he try a little sandpaper, and Pinocchio skipped away enlightened.

A couple of weeks later, Gepetto saw Pinocchio bouncing happily through town and asked him, "How's the girlfriend?"

Pinocchio replied,

"Who needs a girlfriend?" ☺

Cinderella wants to go to the ball, but her wicked stepmother won't let her.

As Cinderella sits crying in the garden, her fairy godmother appears, and promises to provide Cinderella with everything she needs to go to the ball, but only on two conditions. "First, you must wear a diaphragm."

Cinderella agrees. "What's the second condition?"

"You must be home by 2 a.m. Any later, and your diaphragm will turn into a pumpkin."

Cinderella agrees to be home by 2 a.m. The appointed hour comes and goes, and Cinderella doesn't show up.

Finally, at 5 a.m., Cinderella shows up, looking love-struck and **very** satisfied.

"Where have you been?" demands the fairy godmother.

"Your diaphragm was supposed to turn into a pumpkin three hours ago!!!"

"I met a prince, Fairy Godmother. He took care of everything."

"I know of no prince with that kind of power! Tell me his name!"

"I can't remember, exactly... Peter, Peter, something or other..."
☺

A woman was in a coma. She had been in it for months. Nurses were in her room giving her a sponge bath. One of them was washing her private area and noticed that there was a slight response on the monitor when she touched her.

They tried it again and sure enough there was definite movement.

They went to her husband and explained what happened, telling him, "As crazy as this sounds, maybe a little oral sex will do the trick and bring her out of the coma."

The husband was skeptical, but they assured him that they'd close the curtains for privacy. The husband finally agreed and went into his wife's room.

After a few minutes the woman's monitor flat lined, no pulse, no heart rate. The nurses run back into the room.

"What happened!?" they cried.

The husband said,

"I'm not sure - I think maybe she choked" ☺

A man walks into a bar and orders a drink and immediately upon finishing it, reaches into his chest pocket and glares at something, then orders another drink.

This happens 6 times running, and as the bar tender gave him his seventh drink he says to the man,

"What's with this looking at something in your pocket after you finish every drink, if you don't mind telling me?"

"Oh, it's a picture of my wife. I will go home when she starts to look good" ☺

PART 5:
BLOND JOKES

Why is it that blondes get picked on so much? I don't know I just go with it! Hehe

Maybe it is because it is our way of dealing with our insecurities about blondes; or maybe it is because "blondes have more fun" and this is our way to get back at them; or maybe blonds are on average more ditzy than the rest of us, who knows? I am not here for psychoanalyzing, I am here to make you more funny and charming and confident through great joke telling.

So enjoy the best blond jokes I have ever heard (and if you are complaining that this eBook doesn't have enough jokes making fun of Polish people for being stereotypically dumb (I am part Polish so I can say this) then remove "blond" and insert "Polish person" on certain of the jokes below. *As long as you are not Polish or Blond you should be able to figure out which ones to use - LOL*

What do you call a smart blonde?

A golden retriever ☺

A brunette, a blonde, and a redhead are all in third grade. Who has the biggest boobs?

The blonde, because she's 18 ☺

What did the blonde say when she found out she was pregnant?

"Are you sure it's mine?" ☺

What's the newest paint color on the market?

Blonde. It's not very bright, but it spreads really easy! ☺

A brunette is standing on some train tracks, jumping from rail to rail, saying "21" "21" "21."

A Blonde walks up, sees her and decides to join her.
She also starts jumping from rail to rail, saying "21" "21" "21".

Suddenly, the brunette hears a train whistle and jumps off the tracks just as the Blonde is splattered all over the place.

The Brunette goes back to jumping from rail to rail, counting "22" "22" "22" ☺

How do you get a one-armed blonde out of a tree?

Wave to her ☺

Why did the blonde have bruises around her bellybutton?

Because her boyfriend's blonde, too ☺

A blind man enters a lesbian bar by mistake. He finds his way to a bar stool and orders a drink. After sitting there for a while, he yells to the bartender in a loud voice, "Hey bartender, you wanna hear a dumb blonde joke?" The bar immediately falls deathly quiet.

In a deep, husky voice, the woman next to him says, "Before you tell that joke, sir, I think it is just fair, given that you are blind, that you should know five things:

One: The bartender is a blonde woman.

Two: The bouncer is a blonde woman.

Three: The woman sitting next to me is blonde and is a professional boxer.

Four: The lady to your right is a blonde and is a professional wrestler.

Five: I'm a 6 foot, 200 pound blonde woman with a Ph.D., a black belt in karate, and a very bad attitude!

"Now, think seriously, mister. Do you still want to tell that joke?"

The blind man thinks for a second, shakes his head and says: *"Nah. Not if I'm gonna have to explain it five times..."* ☺

What do the Bermuda Triangle and blondes have in common?

They've both swallowed a lot of semen ☺

Two bowling teams, one of all Blondes and one of all Brunettes, charter a double-decker bus for a weekend bowling tournament in Atlantic City. The Brunette team rides in the bottom of the bus. The Blonde team rides on the top level..

The Brunette team down below is whooping it up having a great time, when one of them realizes she doesn't hear anything from the Blondes upstairs. She decides to go up and investigate. When the Brunette reaches the top, she finds all the Blondes frozen in fear, staring straight-ahead at the road, and clutching the seats in front of them with white knuckles..

She says, "What the heck's goin' on up here? We're havin' a grand time downstairs!" One of the Blondes from the second team looks up and says, *"Yeah, but you've got a driver!"* ☺

What is a blondes' idea of safe sex?

A cushion on the headboard ☺

A blonde calls Delta Airlines and asks, "Can you tell me how long it'll take to fly from San Francisco to New York City?"

The agent replies, "Just a minute..."

"Thank you," the blonde says, and hangs up ☺

This dumb blond video is hilarious:
BlondeStar Video/Main Info

http://www.ifilm.com/ifilmdetail/2681355

A painting contractor was speaking with a woman about her job. In the first room she said she would like a pale blue. The contractor wrote this down and went to the window, opened it, and yelled out "GREEN SIDE UP!"

In the second room she told the painter she would like it painted in a soft yellow. He wrote this on his pad, walked to the window, opened it, and yelled "GREEN SIDE UP!" The lady was somewhat curious but she said nothing.

In the third room she said she would like it painted a warm rose color. The painter wrote this down, walked over to the window, opened it and yelled "GREEN SIDE UP!" The lady then asked him, "Why do you keep yelling 'green side up'?"

The contractor replied, *"I'm sorry, but I have a crew of blondes laying sod across the street"* ☺

What do a Boeing 747 and a bleached blonde have in common?

They both have black boxes ☺

There was this beautiful blonde woman in the back of a movie theater doing what appeared to be fingering herself. A man saw this and asked if she could use an extra hand. She is a little embarrassed, but lets the guy eat her out and finger her.

The guy finished his job and return to his seat. A few minutes later the blonde is back at it again. The guy asked her "Was it not good enough for you?" She replies, *"Yes it was. But it's these damn crabs that won't quit itching."* ☺

Why aren't blondes good cattle herders?

Because they can't even keep two calves together! ☺

How do you keep a blonde busy all day?

Put her in a round room and tell her to sit in the corner ☺

How did the blonde die ice fishing?

She was run over by the zamboni machine ☺

What do you do when a blonde throws a pin at you?

Run....she's got a hand grenade in her mouth ☺

What do you call a blonde golfer with an IQ of 125?

A foursome ☺

How do you make a blonde laugh on Saturday?

Tell her a joke on Wednesday ☺

What is the blonde doing when she holds her hands tightly over her ears?

Trying to hold on to a thought ☺

Why did the blonde stare at frozen orange juice can for 2 hours?

Because it said 'concentrate' ☺

Why did the blonde climb up to the roof of the bar?

She heard that the drinks were on the house ☺

Why do blondes work seven days a week?

So you don't have to retrain them on Monday ☺

What is the difference between blondes and traffic signs?

Some traffic signs say stop ☺

What do UFO's and smart blondes have in common?

You keep hearing about them, but never see any ☺

Why do blondes hate M&Ms?

They're too hard to peel ☺

How do you know when a blonde has been making chocolate chip cookies?

You find M&M shells all over the kitchen floor ☺

What job function does a blonde have in an M&M factory?

Proofreading ☺

Do you know why the blonde got fired from the M&M factory?

For throwing out the W's ☺

How do you keep a blonde busy?

Write 'Please turn over' on both sides of a piece of paper ☺

What's brown and red and black and blue?

A brunette who's told one too many blonde jokes ☺

How does the blonde car pool work?

They all meet at work at 7:45 ☺

How did the blonde try to kill the bird?

She threw it off a cliff ☺

How did the blonde break her leg raking leaves?

She fell out of the tree ☺

How did the blonde die drinking milk?

The cow fell on her ☺

How can you tell if a blonde's been using the computer?

There's white-out on the screen ☺

How can you tell when a FAX had been sent from a blonde?

There is a stamp on it ☺

Why is it good to have a blonde passenger?

You can park in the handicap zone ☺

Why do blondes have see-through lunch box lids?

So that when they're on the train they can tell if they're going to work or coming home ☺

Why do men like blonde jokes??

Because they can understand them ☺

Why do blondes like lightning?

They think someone is taking their picture ☺

Why do blondes drive BMWs?

Because they can spell it ☺

What does the postcard from a blonde's vacation say?

Having a wonderful time. Where am I? ☺

Why do Blondes have TGIF on their shoes?

Toes go in first ☺

Why don't blondes call 911 in an emergency?

She can't find the number 11 on the telephone buttons ☺

What does a blonde make best for dinner?

Reservations ☺

What does a blonde say when she gives birth?

Gee, Are you sure it's mine?

What does a blonde say when you ask her if her blinker is on?

It's on. It's off. It's on. It's off. It's on. It's off. ☺

What do you get when you offer a blonde a penny for her thoughts?

Change ☺

What do you call a blonde with half a brain?

Gifted! ☺

What do you call a brunette with a blonde on either side?

An interpreter ☺

What do you call it when a blonde dies their hair brunette?

Artificial intelligence ☺

What do you do when a blonde throws a hand grenade at you?

Pull the pin and throw it back ☺

Why did the blonde scale the chain-link fence?

To see what was on the other side ☺

Why did the blonde keep a coat hanger in her back seat?

In case she locks the keys in her car ☺

Why did the blonde want to become a veterinarian?

Because she loved children ☺

Why did the blonde get so excited after she finished her jigsaw puzzle in only 6 months?

Because on the box it said "From 2-4 years" ☺

Why did the blonde call the welfare office?

She wanted to know how to cook food stamps! ☺

Did you hear about the blond skydiver?

She missed the Earth! ☺

A blonde ordered a pizza and the clerk asked if he should cut it in six or twelve pieces.

"Six, please. I could never eat twelve pieces." ☺

Did you hear about the blonde coyote?

Got stuck in a trap, chewed off three legs and was still stuck ☺

Two bored casino dealers are waiting at the craps table. A very attractive blonde woman arrived and bet twenty-thousand dollars ($20,000) on a single roll of the dice.

She said, "I hope you don't mind, but I feel much luckier when I'm completely nude. "With that, she stripped from the neck down, rolled the dice and yelled, "Come on, baby, Mama needs new clothes!" As the dice came to a stop she jumped up and down and squealed...
"YES! YES! I WON, I WON!"

She hugged each of the dealers and then picked up her winnings and her clothes and quickly departed. The dealers stared at each other dumfounded.

Finally, one of them asked, "What did she roll?"

The other answered, "I don't know - I thought you were watching."

The Moral of the Story - Not all blondes are dumb, but all men are men ☺

PART 6: SNAPS!

Snaps are comments made to poke fun at someone else, or even better, to make fun of their mama! These are very predominant in the African-American community, where they take turns snapping on each other until one cannot remember a new one, or messes up and repeats one that was already said! I watched a competition in high school and it was great!

Yo Mama's so Fat....

Yo mama's so fat, when she goes to a buffet she pulls up a chair.

Yo when she goes to a restaurant, she looks at the menu and says "Yes"

Yo mama's so fat, her blood type is "rocky road".

Yo mama's so fat, when she ran away, they had to put her picture on the milk truck.

Yo mama's so fat, when she hauls ass, she has to make two trips.

Yo mama's so fat, when she dances at a club, she makes the band skip.

Yo mama's so fat, on Halloween she trick or treats two houses at a time.

Yo mama's so fat, I had to take a train and two busses just to get on her good side.

Yo mama's so fat, when she ran away, they had to use all four sides of the milk carton.

Yo mama's so fat, she fills up the bath tub, and then she turns on the water.

Yo mama's so fat, they had to grease a door frame and hold a Twinkie on the other side to get her through.

Yo mama's so fat, when she gets in an elevator, it HAS to go down.

Yo mama's so fat, when she was diagnosed with the flesh eating disease, the doctor gave her 5 years to live.

Yo mama's so fat, her picture takes two frames.

Yo mama's so fat, when your dad climbs on top of her, his ears pop.

Yo mama's so fat, every time she wears high heels, she strikes oil.

Yo mama's so fat, her blood type is Ragu.

Yo mama's so fat, when I climbed up on top of her, I burned my ass on the lightbulb.

Yo mama's so fat, the back of her neck looks like a pack of hot-dogs.

Yo mama's so fat, she DJ's for the ice cream truck.

Yo mama's so fat, when she takes a shower, her feet don't get wet.

Yo mama's so fat, she can't wear Dazzey Dukes. She has to wear Boss Hoggs.

Yo mama's so fat, the shadow of her ass weighs 50 pounds.

Yo mama's so fat, the bitch jumped in the air and got stuck.

Yo mama's so fat, she fell in the Grand Canyon and got stuck!

Yo mama's so fat, her lipstick comes in a spray can.

Yo mama's so fat, she sat on a dollar and made change.

Yo mama's so fat, her skates went flat.

Yo mama's so fat, when her beeper goes off people think she is backing up.

Yo mama's so fat, when she was born, she didn't get a birth certificate, she got blue prints.

Yo Mama's so ugly…

Yo mama's so ugly, her shadow quit.

Yo mama's so ugly, she could only be Yo mama.

Yo mama's so ugly, they filmed "Gorillas in the Mist" in her shower.

Yo mama's so ugly, they push her face into dough to make gorilla cookies.

Yo mama's so ugly, when she looks in the mirror, the reflection ducks.

Yo mama's so ugly, her birth certificate was an apology letter from the condom factory.

Yo mama's so ugly, she looks like she's been in a dryer filled with rocks.

Yo mama's so ugly, she looks like her face caught on fire and they put it out with a fork.

Yo mama's so ugly, her mom had to be drunk to breastfeed her.

Yo mama's so ugly, she couldn't get laid in a prison with a handful of pardons.

Yo mama's so ugly, when she moved into the projects, all her neighbors chipped in for curtains.

Yo mama's so ugly, they rub tree branches on her face to make ugly sticks.

Yo mama's so ugly, her mama had to tie a steak around her neck to get the dog to play with her.

Yo mama's so ugly, even the tide won't take her out.

Yo mama's so ugly, people go as her for Halloween.

Yo mama's so ugly, when she cries, tears run down the back of her neck.

Yo mama's so ugly, she has to creep up on her makeup.

Yo mama was such an ugly baby, her parents had to feed her with a slingshot.

Yo mama's so stupid...

Yo mama's so stupid, she spent twenty minutes lookin' at an orange juice box because it said "concentrate".

Yo mama's so stupid, she put lipstick on her forehead because she wanted to makeup her mind.

Yo mama's so stupid, she thought Grape Nuts was an STD.

Yo mama's so stupid, she saw a billboard that said "Dodge Trucks" and she started ducking through traffic.

Yo mama's so stupid, she uses Old Spice for cooking.

Yo mama's so stupid, she thinks sexual battery is something in a dildo.

Yo mama's so stupid, the first time she used a vibrator, she cracked her two front teeth.

Yo mama's so stupid, when she took you to the airport and a sign said "Airport Left," she turned around and went home.

Yo mama's so stupid, she thought she could get food stamps at the post office.

Yo mama's so stupid that under "Education" on her job application, she put "Hooked on Phonics."

Yo mama's so stupid, it takes her 2 hours to watch 60 Minutes.

Yo mama's so stupid, on her job application where it says emergency contact she put 911.

Yo mama's so old…

Yo mama's so old, I told her to act her age and the bitch died.

Yo mama's so old, she owes Fred Flintstone a food stamp.

Yo mama's so old, the key on Ben Franklin's kite was to her apartment.

Yo mama's so old, her memory is in black and white.

Yo mama's so old, her social security number is 1.

Yo mama's so old, her birth-certificate expired.

Yo mama's so old, she has a picture of Jesus in her yearbook.

Yo mama's so old, she knew Mr. Clean when he had an afro.

Yo mama's so old, she's got Jesus' beeper number.

Yo mama's so old, when she was in school there was no history class.

Yo mama's so old, when she reads the bible she reminisces.

Yo mama's so old, when she was born, the Dead Sea was just getting sick.

Yo mama's so old, she called the cops when David and Goliath started to fight.

Yo mama's so old, she carpooled with Jesus.

PART 7: ETC. – MORE FUNNY STUFF

Items I have enjoyed in the past, hope you like 'em!

If Bud Abbott and Lou Costello were alive today, their infamous sketch, "Who's on first?" might have turned out something like this:

COSTELLO CALLS TO BUY A COMPUTER FROM ABBOTT
ABBOTT: Super Duper computer store. Can I help you?
COSTELLO: Thanks. I'm setting up an office in my den and I'm thinking about buying a computer.
ABBOTT: Mac?
COSTELLO: No, the name's Lou.
ABBOTT: Your computer?
COSTELLO: I don't own a computer. I want to buy one.
ABBOTT: Mac?
COSTELLO: I told you, my name's Lou.
ABBOTT: What about Windows?
COSTELLO: Why? Will it get stuffy in here?
ABBOTT: Do you want a computer with Windows?
COSTELLO: I don't know. What will I see when I look at the windows?
ABBOTT: Wallpaper.
COSTELLO: Never mind the windows. I need a computer and software.
ABBOTT: Software for Windows?
COSTELLO: No. On the computer! I need something I can use to write proposals, track expenses and run my business. What do you have?
ABBOTT: Office.
COSTELLO: Yeah, for my office. Can you recommend anything?
ABBOTT: I just did.
COSTELLO: You just did what?
ABBOTT: Recommend something.

COSTELLO: You recommended something?

ABBOTT: Yes.

COSTELLO: For my office?

ABBOTT: Yes.

COSTELLO: OK, what did you recommend for my office?

ABBOTT: Office.

COSTELLO: Yes, for my office!

ABBOTT: I recommend Office with Windows.

COSTELLO: I already have an office with windows! OK, let's just say I'm sitting at my computer and I want to type a proposal. What do I need?

ABBOTT: Word.

COSTELLO: What word?

ABBOTT: Word in Office.

COSTELLO: The only word in office is office.

ABBOTT: The Word in Office for Windows.

COSTELLO: Which word in office for windows?

ABBOTT: The Word you get when you click the blue "W".

COSTELLO: I'm going to click your blue "W" if you don't start with some straight answers. OK, forget that. Can I watch movies on the Internet?

ABBOTT: Yes, you want Real One.

COSTELLO: Maybe a real one, maybe a cartoon. What I watch is none of your business. Just tell me what I need!

ABBOTT: Real One.

COSTELLO: If it's a long movie, I also want to watch reels 2, 3 and 4. Can I watch them?

ABBOTT: Of course.

COSTELLO: Great! With what?

ABBOTT: Real One.

COSTELLO: OK, I'm at my computer and I want to watch a movie. What do I do?

ABBOTT: You click the blue "1".

COSTELLO: I click the blue one what?

ABBOTT: The blue "1".

COSTELLO: Is that different from the blue "W"?

ABBOTT: The blue "1" is Real One and the blue "W" is Word.

COSTELLO: What word?

ABBOTT: The Word in Office for Windows.

COSTELLO: But there are three words in "office for windows"!

ABBOTT: No, just one. But it's the most popular Word in the world.

COSTELLO: It is?

ABBOTT: Yes, but to be fair, there aren't many other Words left. It pretty much wiped out all the other words out there.

COSTELLO: And that word is real one?

ABBOTT: Real One has nothing to do with Word. Real One isn't even part of Office.

COSTELLO: STOP! Don't start that again. What about financial bookkeeping? You have anything I can track my money with?

ABBOTT: Money.

COSTELLO: That's right. What do you have?

ABBOTT: Money.

COSTELLO: I need money to track my money?

ABBOTT: It comes bundled with your computer.

COSTELLO: What's bundled with my computer?

ABBOTT: Money.

COSTELLO: Money comes with my computer?

ABBOTT: Yes. No extra charge.

COSTELLO: I get a bundle of money with computer. How much?

ABBOTT: One copy.

COSTELLO: Isn't it illegal to copy money?

ABBOTT: Microsoft gave us a license to copy Money.

COSTELLO: They can give you a license to copy money?

ABBOTT: Why not? THEY OWN IT! (A few days later)

ABBOTT: Super Duper computer store. Can I help you?

COSTELLO: How do I turn my computer off?

ABBOTT: Click on "START"...

Prison vs. Work

Just in case you ever get these two environments mixed up, this should make things a little bit clearer.

IN PRISON..........you spend the majority of your time in an 10x10 cell.

AT WORK............you spend the majority of your time in an 8x8 cubicle.

IN PRISON.........you get three meals a day.

AT WORK...........you get a break for one meal and you have to pay for it.

IN PRISON.........you get time off for good behavior.

AT WORK...........you get more work for good behavior.

IN PRISON..........the guard locks and unlocks all the doors for you.

AT WORK............you must carry a security card and open all the doors for yourself.

IN PRISON..........you can watch TV and play games.

AT WORK...........you could get fired for watching TV and playing games.

IN PRISON.........you get your own toilet.

AT WORK..........you have to share the toilet with some people who pee on the seat.

IN PRISON..........they allow your family and friends to visit.

AT WORK...........you aren't even supposed to speak to your family.

IN PRISON..........all expenses are paid by the taxpayers with no work required.

AT WORK...........you get to pay all your expenses to go to work, and they deduct taxes from your salary to pay for prisoners.

IN PRISON..........you spend most of your life inside bars wanting to get out.

AT WORK ....you spend most of your time wanting to get out and go inside bars.

IN PRISON ....you must deal with sadistic wardens.

AT WORK..........they are called managers.

Now get back to work. You're not getting paid to check emails!

And some Women Bashing:

I married Miss Right. I just didn't know her first name was Always.

In the beginning, G-d created earth and rested. Then G-d created man and rested. Then G-d created woman.
Since then, neither G-d nor man has rested.

Why do men die before their wives? They want to.

Do you know the punishment for bigamy? Two mothers-in-law.

How do most men define marriage? An expensive way to get laundry done for free.

Then there was a man who said, "I never knew what real happiness was until I got married; and then it was too late."

Marriage is a 3-ring circus: Engagement ring, wedding ring, and suffering.

Answering machine at the mental hospital:

"Hello, and welcome to the mental health hotline"

-If you are obsessive-compulsive, press 1 repeatedly.
-If you are co-dependent, please ask someone to press 2 for you.
-If you have multiple personalities, press 3, 4, 5, and 6.
-If you are paranoid, we know who you are and what you want. Stay on the line so we can trace your call.
-If you are delusional, press 7 and your call will be transferred to the mother ship.

-If you are schizophrenic, listen carefully and a small voice will tell you which number to press.

-If you are a manic-depressive, it doesn't matter which number you press, no one will answer.

-If you are dyslexic, press 9696969696969696.

-If you have a nervous disorder, please fidget with the # key until a representative comes on the line.

-If you have amnesia, press 8 and state your name, address, phone number, date of birth, social security number, and your mother's maiden name.

-If you have post-traumatic stress disorder, s-l-o-w-l-y & c-a-r-e-f-u-l-l-y press 0 0 0.

-If you have bipolar disorder, please leave a message after the beep or before the beep or after the beep. Please wait for the beep.

-If you have short-term memory loss, press 9.

-If you have short-term memory loss, press 9.

-If you have short-term memory loss, press 9.

-If you have short-term memory loss, press 9.

-If you have low self-esteem, please hang up. All operators are too busy to talk to you.

-If you are blonde don't press any buttons, you'll just screw it up.

FUNNY BECAUSE IT'S TRUE:

If I ever become an Evil Overlord:

1. My legions of terror will have helmets with clear plexiglass visors, not face-concealing ones.

2. My ventilation ducts will be too small to crawl through.

3. My noble half-brother whose throne I usurped will be killed, not kept anonymously imprisoned in a forgotten cell of my dungeon.

4. Shooting is not too good for my enemies.

5. The artifact which is the source of my power will not be kept on the Mountain of Despair beyond the River of Fire guarded by the Dragons of Eternity. It will be in my safe-deposit box.

6. I will not gloat over my enemies' predicament before killing them.

7. When the rebel leader challenges me to fight one-on-one and asks, "Or are you afraid without your armies to back you up?" My reply will be, "No, just sensible."

8. When I've captured my adversary and he says, "Look, before you kill me, will you at least tell me what this is all about?" I'll say, "Nope" and shoot him.

9. After I kidnap the beautiful princess, we will be married immediately in a quiet civil ceremony, not a lavish spectacle in three weeks time during which the final phase of my plan will be carried out.

10. I will not include a self-destruct mechanism unless absolutely necessary. If it is necessary, it will not be a large red button labeled "Danger: Do Not Push".

11. I will not order my trusted lieutenant to kill the infant who is destined to overthrow me -- I'll do it myself.

12. I will not interrogate my enemies in the inner sanctum -- a small hotel well outside my borders will work just as well.

13. I will be secure in my superiority. Therefore, I will feel no need to prove it by leaving clues in the form of riddles or leaving my weaker enemies alive to show they pose no threat.

14. I will make it clear that I do know the meaning of the word "mercy"; I simply choose not show them any.

15. One of my advisors will be an average five-year-old child. Any flaws in my plan that he is able to spot will be corrected before its implementation.

16. My undercover agents will not have tattoos identifying them as members of my organization, nor will they be required to wear military boots or adhere to any other dress codes.

17. The hero is not entitled to a last kiss, a last cigarette, or any other form of last request.

18. I will never employ any device with a digital countdown.

If I find that such a device is absolutely unavoidable, I will set it to activate when the counter reaches 117 and the hero is just putting his plan into operation.

19. I will design all doomsday machines myself. If I must hire a mad scientist to assist me, I will make sure that he is sufficiently twisted to never regret his evil ways and seek to undo the damage he's caused.

20. I will never utter the sentence "But before I kill you, there's just one thing I want to know."

21. When I employ people as advisors, I will occasionally listen to their advice.

PART 8:
SPECIAL BONUS SECTION!
THE FUNNIEST SITES ON THE WEB!!!

If you are like me, not only do you get jokes, some funny, some not so funny, but you also get a number of forwards from your friends and family. Some people send me way too many forwards. Just like I only send the best jokes I receive, I only forward the funniest forwards I receive.

Here is a bunch of links to really funny things I have seen on the Internet and really great websites as well that I have previously forwarded in my Friday Funnies.

HILARIOUS DANCER:

When you have 6 minutes free, this comedian dancing is hilarious (I think he has his own show now out of this): http://www.youtube.com/watch?v=dMH0bHeiRNg

RODNEY DANGERFIELD'S WEBSITE:

http://www.rodney.com/rodney/home/home.asp

EBAUMS WORLD:

http://www.ebaumsworld.com

PHONE NUMBER TRICK:

This cool site tells you what your phone number spells:
http://www22.verizon.com/Vanity/SrcFiles/VtMain/

THATSCOMEDY.COM:

www.thatscomedy.com

WIDGETS FOR YOUR COMPUTER:

This is cool! Get widgets for you computer!
http://www.konfabulator.com/

FUNNY:

http://video.yahoo.com/video/play?vid=c618bf049cd34ff9fb4532cdcf2
3c0e4.635579

FUNNY:

http://www.ebaumsworld.com/flash/cursortheft.html

6 DEGREES OF KEVIN BACON:

http://www.cs.virginia.edu/oracle/

SAMURAI KITTENS

If you want to waste some time, here is a game for that -
http://www.samuraikittens.com/

THE DILDO SONG:

http://revver.com/video/1827/

MYSPACE, THE MOVIE:

THIS IS HILARIOUS (10 MINUTES LONG) -
http://www.youtube.com/watch?v=nFT-
lyFN3BM&feature=Views&page=1&t=a&f=b

ZOOASS.COM:

www.zooass.com

SICKO "MARRIAGE CONTRACT":

If you haven't heard of the crazy marriage contract it is hysterical!
When you have a few minutes it is a must read!
http://www.thesmokinggun.com/archive/0217062contract1.html?link=e
af

AMAZING SHIRT FOLDING TECHNIQUE:

FOLD T-SHIRTS QUICKLY AND EASILY!
http://video.yahoo.com/video/play?vid=39ebc2419a791ea5ea16a753e4abc9
6d.686246&cache=1

MILLIONDOLLAR HOMEPAGE:

A young guy in London made a million dollars with this –

http://www.milliondollarhomepage.com

CARD STACKER:

The best card stacker in the world!
http://www.cardstacker.com/index2.html

How did the electrician lose all the power in his home?
He got married! ☺

THE END

**For more great books please visit
www.OutstandingeBooks.com**